THE AMULEK
ALTERNATIVE

THE AMULEK ALTERNATIVE

Exercising Agency in a World of Choice

Anne Osborn Poelman

Deseret Book Company
Salt Lake City, Utah

Interior photos © M. Yamashito, Westlight.
Used by permission.

Library of Congress Cataloging-in-Publication Data
Poelman, Anne Osborn, 1943–
    The Amulek alternative / by Anne Osborn Poelman.
        p.   cm.
    Includes index.
    ISBN 1-57345-322-6 (hardbound)
    1. Free will and determinism—Religious aspects—Mormon Church.
2. Spiritual life—Mormon Church.   3. Amulek (Book of Mormon figure).
4. Mormon Church—Doctrines.   5. Church of Jesus Christ of Latter-day
Saints—Doctrines.   6. Poelman, Anne Osborn, 1943–
I. Title.
BX8643.F69P64   1997
248.4'89332—dc21
                                                                    97-28687
                                                                        CIP

Printed in the United States of America
10 9   8   7   6   5   4   3   2   1   72082

For Laurel

Contents

Contents

Preface

"Are you going to write a sequel to *The Simeon Solution?*" I've been asked.

Well, not exactly.

The Amulek Alternative isn't a "sequel," at least not in the contemporary meaning of the word. I hope it's not like some movies that seem to keep going on and on, each one a paler imitation of its predecessor. This book doesn't begin where *The Simeon Solution* ended, either.

The idea for *The Amulek Alternative* arose from my growing concern that many people today feel their lives are spinning out of control, swept along by events that are far beyond their own influence. There always seem to be too many competing choices, too many attractive alternatives. Drifting passively with popular currents, people may easily slip by the most crucial decision points in their lives, unaware of their importance. Decisions are made by default. Nonchoice, in essence, becomes a choice.

On the other hand, if we are spiritually in tune, we can recognize the points at which life's pathways diverge. We can know which road will lead us toward our eternal goals and a happier, more fulfilled life. *That* road is often the less-traveled, more obscure path.

Much of life is about choosing. We have been given the precious gift of agency, the capacity to choose our own path. *We* can decide for ourselves what we will do and who we will become.

An integral part of agency is accountability, meaning we are also responsible for our choices. We can, if we so determine, choose wisely and well. But it is all too easy to become distracted from our eternal goals, to make choices based on worldly values. One of our goals in mortality should be to learn to base our decisions on revealed truth and a knowledge of God's plan for us, as opposed to the ever-changing popular philosophies of the day.

Amulek, one of the less well-known prophets in the Book of Mormon, was an individual who, in the world's terms, "had it all." Yet somehow he knew—at least subconsciously—that something was missing. When at last he came to *the* most critical decision point of his life, he found the courage to take the less-traveled road.

And that, as the poet Robert Frost said, made all the difference.

Nancy Packer, an emeritus Professor of English at Stanford University who served for many years as director of the creative writing program, often told her students, "You must have a moral center from which the art radiates." My viewpoints come straight from the core of very traditional values. To some they may seem remarkably conservative. I make no apologies for that. I am rooted and firmly grounded in the values which I learned as a child and which have been refined and amplified by my chosen religion.

The stories and discussions I've included in *The Amulek Alternative* are, for the most part, about real people and real events. All are about exercising agency and accepting accountability in a world full of choices.

INTRODUCTION
The Amulek Alternative

People everywhere yearn to believe. We want to find meaning in our increasingly frenetic, fragmented lives. Just being successful—as the world defines it—is not enough. We feel there should be, there *must* be, something more to life.

More than a millennium ago an ancient American prophet named Amulek found himself in a strikingly similar situation. Deep within his soul he knew, although he was reluctant to acknowledge it, that there was something missing.

Amulek found it. We can too.

Chapter 1

Turning Point

Robert permitted himself the delicious luxury of a small smile. Not a big guffaw, of course, or even a broad grin. Given his position and reputation in the community, such a display of self-indulgence would have been inappropriate—perhaps even unseemly.

As he strolled through the central square, the nods of recognition and deferential greetings from neighbors and even strangers added to his considerable pleasure. Robert—known as "Rob" to his family and the small handful of business associates who were both successful and presumptive enough to assume a first-name basis—was secure in the satisfying knowledge that even if he didn't know everyone who greeted him by name, they certainly knew who *he* was.

Robert always returned the many admiring but respectful salutations with carefully calibrated modesty—a slight inclination of the head here, a short wave of the hand there. To those few whom he regarded as his true peers, a warm but brief handclasp was in order.

All in all, it was a very fine day indeed. So nice that he decided to treat himself to a few rare moments alone.

Detouring into a nearby park, Robert sank down on a bench

for a brief respite. The impending visit with one of his close kindred—a family duty that as the unspoken patriarch of the clan he cheerfully shouldered—could wait.

He frowned.

The nagging unease was back.

He hated that now-familiar but unwelcome feeling. It disturbed the cherished sense of well-being he had nurtured so assiduously. As on many previous occasions, he tried to push the restlessness back into the far recesses of his mind. Unlike those earlier times, the uneasy feeling simply wouldn't cooperate. It refused to disappear.

Robert would have been hard put to describe exactly what was bothering him. It was . . . nameless. Every time he tried to pin the feeling down, it eluded him. But it was always there, lurking around the distant edges of his consciousness and eroding his much-valued peace of mind.

He tried one of his old mental tricks: Look on the bright side. Accentuate the positive. Dismiss the negative. Robert mentally rehearsed his array of accomplishments. His professional stature and considerable reputation were enviable. He counted numerous influential and famous people among his friends and acquaintances. He was rich, not just your average, run-of-the-mill rich, but *really* rich. Best of all, he'd made his fortune himself. His father had left him their distinguished family name and lineage but little else. The money had come as the reward of Robert's own unrelenting hard work.

Except for a never-ending struggle with weight, Robert was in excellent health. His wife was a handsome woman who still turned heads when they walked into the dining room at the club. The children—growing up too fast, as children do—were popular and doing well in school.

What more could a guy possibly want? Robert thought to himself for the umpteenth time. *I've got everything I ever dreamed would make me happy. Why do I feel unsatisfied, so empty inside?*

Turning his face toward the brassy midday sun, Robert shut his eyes with a grateful sigh. That was better. The sun's glow gradually seeped through his tightly closed eyelids, a riot of color and swirling patterns of light that nudged his overtired brain toward the precipice of sleep.

He suddenly started, jolted from somnolence by the distinct feeling that someone was quietly watching him. In itself, that wasn't unusual; he was used to being observed closely. Partially blinded by the bright sun, he stood up and slowly peered around the park.

No one.

Still, he had the eerie feeling he wasn't alone. As his eyes gradually readjusted, he scanned the park again.

Empty.

He was *certain.* Someone was there.

Behind him.

Afraid to turn, he froze. He actually felt the hairs on the back of his neck rise.

Then he heard it, so softly, so sweetly he almost believed it was his imagination.

His name.

He turned as the gentle but irresistible voice banished his fears. The radiant figure standing behind him made the sunlight seem weak, almost insubstantial. A wildly irrational thought crossed Robert's mind: *I wish I'd watched that TV program Sarah and the kids like so much.*

As though it could read his thoughts, the figure waited silently until Robert's confused mind cleared. Then it spoke.

"Go home," the figure commanded. "Prepare yourself and your family to receive a very special guest. He is a holy man, a prophet of the Lord. He has been chosen by God Himself to teach the people. He has fasted many days in preparation and is hungry. You will feed him and listen to him. You will heed his counsel. And he will bless you and all your house."

Years later, Rob would recount this story, his voice still filled with wonder at the memory. And, despite the considerable sacrifices and intervening hardships, he always spoke without regret or reservation.

"I really thought I had it all: money, reputation, family. I'd worked hard and deserved it, or so I told myself. Despite everything, in the back of my mind I guess I always knew there was something missing.

"I suppose I'd always believed in God, but I mostly ignored those feelings. Church was a matter of convenience—mostly inconvenience, at that! I was too busy expanding the business. There never seemed to be enough time. So I just kept on going, until one day . . .

"I didn't really believe all that crackpot, hokey stuff. You know, being 'touched by an angel' or having dreams or visions. But it actually happened. To me! It changed my whole life. I could have ignored the figure or dismissed the whole episode as my imagination. But it was real.

"I went home. And the man came, just as the figure had said. He taught. I listened. I knew instinctively that what he said was true. And I've been sharing that message ever since."

Robert is, of course, a figment of my own imagination, a completely fictional Everyman. But Amulek, one of the ancient American prophets in the Book of Mormon, is not. His is a true story. A well-known and wealthy man in his own community, Amulek came from a distinguished family and had accomplished much. He had a comfortable life. In his own words, he tells us:

> I never have known much of the ways of the Lord, and his mysteries and marvelous power. I said I never had known much of these things; but behold, I mistake, for I have seen much of his mysteries and his marvelous power; yea, even in the preservation of the lives of this people.
>
> Nevertheless, I did harden my heart, for I was called many times and I would not hear; therefore I knew concerning these things, yet I would not know; therefore I went on rebelling against God . . .
>
> —Alma 10:5–6

Amulek *knew,* yet he would not know. For a long time he resisted his feelings. But when at last he came to the critical turning point of his life, he made the right decision.

Many of us, myself included, have had similar feelings. We often *know,* but don't yet consciously recognize, that there is more to life than we are currently experiencing or are willing to admit to ourselves. We sense that being successful—at least in conventional terms—is somehow not enough. We feel an insistent inner yearning, a longing that comes from the deepest wellsprings of our souls.

We silently ask, *Is there more to life?* and desperately hope that indeed there is. We may also instinctively resist those feelings. After all, change is often inconvenient and almost always unsettling.

Like Amulek, we all face crucial decision points that may change our lives forever. Amulek's timeless example leaps from the pages of scriptures. He answers our heartfelt queries with a resounding example of faith, commitment, and perseverance. Yes, he assures us from the perspective of his own experience, there is indeed an eternally more rewarding path, harder though it may be.

Amulek's alternative was to choose—and then to endure—the less-traveled road.

Chapter 2

The "R" Word

Warm, humid air gave the semitropical night an almost velvety feeling. The soft, rhythmic clatter of palm fronds rustling in the breeze added to the moment's enjoyment. Relishing the precious moments of solitude after an intense international medical imaging conference, I stood on the balcony and gazed out at the bustling city. Five-star hotels and luxury high-rises formed a glittering necklace of lights that adorned the distant bay.

My reverie was short-lived. A group of colleagues quickly gathered, interrupting my musings to chat about the meeting.

Tantalizing aromas drifted on the evening air as everyone attacked trays of savory appetizers. I tried not to talk with my mouth full. Rude, my mother would have said. But I was famished and knew the food on the long, grueling overnight flight that still awaited would pale in comparison.

I almost choked in surprise when without warning one of my colleagues turned to me and asked, "Dr. Osborn, do you believe in God?"

All conversation suddenly stopped.

I swallowed hastily and answered without hesitation, "Yes. Absolutely."

It may have been just my imagination, but in the semidarkness I thought I saw looks of wistful envy on several faces.

"How do you know? How can you really *know* God exists?" one asked somewhat anxiously.

I have always thought that to one who believes, no proof is necessary, and to one who doesn't, none is sufficient. But I was searching for an answer that might be more helpful, something that would bridge the cultural gulf and differences in religious background that almost certainly lay between us.

Finally I said: "I think the feeling that God exists comes from the accumulation of lots of different experiences. Small ones as well as big ones. For example, I believe that God hears—in fact, *has* heard—my personal, private prayers and has answered them on any number of occasions."

"God has answered your prayers? What do you pray for?" another colleague inquired skeptically.

"Oh, it varies. Sometimes I don't ask Him for anything at all; I just express gratitude for my blessings and opportunities. At other times, I've asked for help with very specific decisions. Some are major, such as whether to become a Mormon, which job to take, and whether or not I should marry Ron." Those listeners who knew my husband from our previous visits to India smiled at the last choice and its obvious answer.

I continued, "I also pray about relatively small problems, like when I have the occasional really difficult diagnostic dilemma at the hospital. Perhaps it's something that I've never seen before, not in thousands and thousands of cases."

There were nods at that one. Everyone had been in similar situations.

"So what do you do?" another inquired. "How do you go about getting an answer for a particularly tough case?"

"I ask the Lord to help me notice the pertinent findings and perceive other, sometimes subtle, abnormalities that might provide a clue to the case. I often ask Him to help me recall having read about similar problems, even in an obscure journal article or case report that I may have seen years before. Most of the time it works."

"And if it doesn't?"

"Then I ask for the wisdom and inspiration to send the case to someone else who might know what it is and what to do about it. No one knows everything," I assured them.

The discussion was interrupted by a call from our host to come inside for dinner. I lingered behind on the balcony, reluctant to leave the intriguing conversation. Ravi Ramakantan, one of our best friends and a highly respected Hindu colleague, had been quietly observing the unusual interchange.

"Anne, they really love and respect you," he commented, to my embarrassment. "Who you are, what you think, and that you are comfortable with letting them know how you feel inside is really important to them. That someone like you is a 'believer' means something very special. It gives them—well, *hope*."

One of my husband's former business colleagues had once said something similar to him, remarking, "I don't believe what you believe. I don't think I could live as you do. But the fact that *you* believe and live right gives *me* hope."

As the global rhythm and pace of life have become increasingly frenetic, people everywhere seem to feel swept along, trapped in a maelstrom of events far beyond their comprehension, let alone their control. As happened with my Indian colleagues, there seems to be a genuine, growing eagerness to discuss deeply meaningful topics of eternal importance.

Though they live in the midst of unprecedented abundance, people are starving for faith. The pop philosophy and junk-food theology regularly served up in the media and preached from pulpits across the land are largely devoid of spiritual nutrition. Like empty calories, they may fill but they don't satisfy.

Traditional values and social anchors have been first ignored, then ridiculed, scorned, and finally discarded altogether, replaced by a watered-down, ethically weak-kneed moral relativism. The proponents of "values-neutral" education—and they are both many and loud—refuse to accept the time-honored but "outmoded" concept that some things are plainly *wrong*, or that others are simply *right*.

I was dismayed to read a recent poll reporting that nearly two in three adult Americans believe that ethics "vary by situation" or that there is no "unchanging ethical standard of right and wrong." Elastic ethics, variable values. You don't have to be a genius to predict the result. Without transcendent standards, behavior that used to be considered unacceptable is redefined as normal and pushed into the cultural mainstream.

Repudiation of the old constraints has had a price, and it is a steep one indeed. Lacking an ethical compass and feeling out of control of their own lives, people put themselves into a passive "drift" mode. It becomes all too easy to float aimlessly with popular currents, allowing oneself to be caught up and carried along by trendy tides.

Individuals who base their behavior on a set of slippery, ever-shifting standards and wobbly reasoning engage in a precarious balancing act. The destructive effect on society as a whole is predictable. President Gordon B. Hinckley recently spoke of his deep concern:

My great concern, my great interest, is that we preserve for the generations to come those wondrous elements of our society and manner of living that will bequeath to them the strengths and the goodness of which we have been the beneficiaries. But I worry as I see some of the signs of sickness of which I have spoken.

I believe that a significant factor in the decay we observe about us comes of a forsaking of the God whom our fathers knew, loved, worshiped and looked to for strength.

There is a plainly discernible secularization that is occurring. Its consequences are a deterioration of family life, a weakening of self-discipline, a scoffing at the thought of accountability unto the Almighty, and an unbecoming arrogance for any people who have been so richly blessed through the goodness of a generous Providence as we have been.

—*Church News,* 5 April 1997

As the turn of the millennium approaches, money is not the only commodity undergoing relentless inflation. Progressively more explicit depictions of sex, terror, fear, brutality, and violence in entertainment and the media numb our sense of perspective. As we lose our capacity for outrage, public behavior itself becomes ever more outrageous. "Do your own thing" and "you deserve a break today" were just the beginning. Where's the end?

In the absence of lofty goals, undisguised materialism is glamorized and even celebrated. "Show me the money!" the star screams as he dances a little on-screen jig of joy for all the world to see. And the world laughs with him.

Modern-day disciples of despair nod in not-so-silent satisfaction. In order for them to rebuild society—in their own image and according to their own blueprints, of course—the old order with its outdated concepts must first be discredited and then thoroughly demolished.

In our so-called post-modern society, religion has become the "R" word, a topic carefully skirted—if not assiduously avoided—in sophisticated, politically correct circles. Among the self-anointed intellectual elite, any mention of religious faith typically elicits uncomfortable looks if not outright scorn. Yet these same individuals see nothing amiss when television ads portray driving a car as a spiritual experience and describe the pleasures of drinking a particular brand of beer in hushed, almost reverential tones.

Secularism and ironic detachment have been In. Expressions of belief and commitment have been most emphatically Out. And yet, there is a pervasive restlessness that many people all around the world are experiencing. A searching. A yearning.

The truth is that people everywhere want to believe, to trust in some kind of divine oversight. They desperately need to have hope. They yearn to feel that Someone is actually in charge of the whole shebang. Perhaps most of all, they want to believe that that Someone is aware of and cares for them—individually, lovingly, and mercifully.

At long last, *something* is stirring in the land. And that stirring is becoming very widespread indeed.

We have come a long way from the sixties when a *Time* magazine cover pondered the rhetorical question, "Is God Dead?" (The conclusion seemed to be that if He wasn't exactly moribund, He surely had "one foot in the grave and the other on a banana peel!") Other chronicles of disbelief in that seminal era eagerly charted the unmaking of core values and the dismantling of moral standards.

By contrast, attention-catching articles in a broad spectrum of newspapers and national magazines today query, "Does Heaven Exist?" (*Time*, 24 March 1997), "Is There Life after Death?" (*U.S.*

News & World Report, 31 March 1997), and "Is God Listening?" (*Newsweek,* 31 March 1997).

Television shows about angels and miracles sit atop the ratings charts. The recent re-release of the Star Wars trilogy set box-office records. I firmly believe its broad audience appeal was not because of the dazzling special effects, which, after all, reflected twenty-year-old technology. But the movies' themes—good versus evil, right against wrong, personal sacrifice and dedication to selfless causes and noble purposes, even forgiveness and redemption—are timeless. In these modern classics, the Enemy has a name and a face. Evil is easily identified and morally unambiguous. Childishly simplistic? I think not.

Some may argue that the interest in spiritual matters is a temporary one. They would have us believe that faith is a trenchant but nonetheless transient topic of conversation. They would likewise dismiss the desire to believe as merely another fad that, like all such passing fancies, will eventually be replaced by some other focus of popular enthusiasm.

They are wrong.

Even lofty citadels of secular humanism are feeling the first faint ripples of spiritual revival. In the March/April 1997 issue of *Stanford Today,* an article titled "Faith Makes a Comeback" declared that a new interest in spirituality was touching academic life in that bastion of political correctness. With thirty-one different religious organizations now on campus, spiritual life at my alma mater is rapidly becoming more pervasive and much more visible. As the consummate institutional barometer and indicator of what's currently in vogue—namely, resources allocated to personnel and staffing—the university's own Memorial Church recently hired three new associate deans for religious life!

In August 1996, the *New York Times* reported that "in a time of outward tension and inner searching, when many Americans worry about social decay and also show a growing interest in spirituality, teachers and administrators on campuses are asking whether colleges ought to try once again to build moral and spiritual character as well as intellect."

Imagine that.

In words that might apply as well to our day as they did to ancient Israel, the prophet Amos foretold: "Behold, the days come, saith the Lord God, that I will send a famine in the land, not a famine of bread, nor a thirst for water, but of hearing the words of the Lord: And they shall wander . . . [and] run to and fro to seek the word of the Lord, and shall not find it." (Amos 8:11-12.)

Other prophets, both ancient and modern, have in simplicity and plainness pointed out the way to a happier, more fulfilling life. Although the moral high road they tirelessly urge us to follow is often an obscure, difficult, and even lonely path, it is ultimately the more rewarding way.

Amulek is a prime example of one who discovered and then chose to follow that less-traveled but better road. In fact, way down deep inside he'd really known the right path all along. But like many of us, for a long time he just wouldn't admit to himself that he knew it. He finally had to commit himself to the eternal values he knew were right.

President Gordon B. Hinckley's counsel to all of us, especially the youth, is straightforward and unmistakable:

> You have been taught many values of divine origin. These values are based on the commandments which the finger of the Lord wrote upon the tablets of stone when Moses spoke with Jehovah upon the mountain. You know them. You are familiar with them.
>
> The values you have been taught likewise are based upon the

beatitudes which Jesus spoke to the multitude. These, with others of His divine teachings, constitute a code of ethics, a code of values . . . . To these have been added the precepts and commandments of modern revelation.

Combined together these basic, divinely given principles must constitute your value system. You cannot escape the consequences of their observance. If you will shape your lives according to their pattern, I do not hesitate to promise that you will know much of peace and happiness, of growth and achievement. To the degree that you fail to observe them, I regretfully say that the fruits will be disappointment, sadness, misery, and even tragedy . . . . I challenge you to rise above the sordid elements of the world about you.

—Conference Report, April 1992, p. 99

There is great joy and satisfaction in choosing right and resisting evil. We should make no mistake about it: Evil *does* exist. Satan is no imaginary adversary. There *is* a right and wrong to just about every question and moral dilemma. My parents taught that; yours probably did too.

Mortality is fundamentally about making choices, especially learning to "choose the right." This life provides us with opportunities to learn and grow by choosing between attractive alternatives and then experiencing the consequences of those decisions. We will stand at many such crossroads.

Our daily choices really *are* significant—in both an immediate and an eternal sense.

THE ROAD DIVIDES
Agency and Opposites

Amulek lived the world's way, succeeding on its terms and reaping its rewards in abundance. Then Alma taught him the Lord's way, and he knew he must choose between his easy, comfortable existence and a better but harder road. Amulek's experiences would reflect, in stark contrast, the extremes of the sublime and the satanic. He had personally seen an angel, yet he would also be forced to watch as innocent women and children were burned alive for their beliefs.

As part of God's plan, each of us is permitted to exercise the divine gift of agency either for good or for evil. Let us make no mistake about it: Evil is real. Satan exists. We can decide to select the wrong. We can also choose the right.

Chapter 3

Laurel

Laurel is the daughter I never had. I really do love her. She is a genuinely *good* person, one of the best I've ever known. She has tried to do the right things her entire life: to help other people, live faithfully, study the scriptures, pray often, and always keep a prayerful heart.

It's always unsettling when bad things happen to good people, especially to those closest to us. I struggle with why Laurel, the youngest of Ron's four children, has had such a difficult life. Her mother was diagnosed with breast cancer when Laurel was only six; Claire died from its complications during Laurel's senior year in high school. Her father, newly called as a General Authority, moved to Salt Lake City just before Laurel left for Brigham Young University.

"Home" during holidays and breaks was no longer their cherished dream house on Longden Circle in the hills of Los Altos, California. Rather than remain cooped up in Ron's impersonal city apartment, Laurel often spent vacations traveling or visiting with friends.

She met and married a spectacularly talented student who was embarking on a career in cosmetic dentistry. After his graduation from dental school, they moved to Los Angeles. Her husband borrowed heavily to set up a practice in Westwood, perhaps hoping to become a "dentist to the stars." A young mother of one, then two, then three beautiful children, Laurel stayed home and finished college with correspondence courses.

The marriage, often rocky, was shaken to its very foundations when Laurel began to suspect—first with disbelief and then with growing concern—that her husband might be using drugs. Drug Enforcement Agency agents began investigating him for alleged prescription violations. Under threat of imminent prosecution, family "crisis intervention" resulted in his admission to first one and then another drug treatment program.

Laurel hung in there as her husband's behavior became increasingly erratic and occasionally even violent. She was eventually left at home to struggle with their three small children by herself. Ron and I spent many tear-filled hours with her, agonizing and praying over her difficult situation.

"Daddy," she would say with grim determination, "I went to the temple and made a solemn covenant. And I'm going to do everything I possibly can to keep it." Neither she nor we mentioned divorce.

One day Ron came home, his face bleak. "Laurel called me at the office this afternoon," he recounted. "I could tell she'd been crying."

Ron was near tears himself. "She said just one word, 'Daddy.' I could hear some small choking sounds. Then there was a long pause as she fought for control. She finally sighed and asked me, 'Daddy, did I agree to this before I came to earth? Did I *know* it would be so hard?'"

I waited as he stopped, struggling for composure himself.

"I finally said to her, 'Yes, dear, you did. We *all* did.'" He continued, "There was another prolonged pause. Then I heard her choke. 'Oh, Daddy,' she said pleadingly, 'Did I shout for joy?'"

Yes, Laurel, you did. And you will again.

God himself has declared, "Men are, that they might have joy" (2 Nephi 2:25) and "This is my work and my glory—to bring to pass the immortality and eternal life of man" (Moses 1:39).

The gospel teaches us that before birth we existed as spirit children of our Father in Heaven. In order to realize a fulness of joy and progress toward our destiny of eternal life, we needed to experience mortality.

Elder Jeffrey R. Holland has summarized the essential role of mortality:

> God's premortal children could not become like him and enjoy his breadth of blessings unless they obtained both a physical body and temporal experience in an arena where both good and evil were present . . . such a temporal experience must be predicated upon moral agency, which includes the moral and intellectual ability to distinguish right from wrong and the attendant freedom to make choices based on that knowledge.
> —*Christ and the New Covenant* (Salt Lake City: Deseret Book, 1997), p. 200

As God's spirit children, we knew that mortality would bring both risks and opportunities. Just how much detail and what specifics of our forthcoming mortal experience we knew in advance isn't really known. However, we did understand that we would be tried and tested in the crucible of life's experiences. We knew that no one would be exempt from either trials or temptations. No one would be immune from pain and suffering.

We recognized that an essential part of our mortal experience would be to exercise the power of choice we call *agency*. There would be real choices between attractive alternatives, what Elder Holland calls "contending enticements."

We also knew we would often make those decisions in the face of opposition (see 2 Nephi 2:16; D&C 29:39). Our choices would, in turn, have real consequences. Some of those consequences would have eternal significance. If we remained faithful and were obedient to God's commandments, we could return to our Father in Heaven to share eternal life and exaltation with Him.

Prophets throughout the ages have called God's design for us by various names, including the "plan of salvation" and "the great plan of happiness" (Alma 42:8). The scriptures record that when this great plan of happiness was presented to us in the premortal existence, we "shouted for joy" (Job 38:7).

As part of the great plan, we would retain no conscious memory of what preceded our birth. Learning to walk by faith would be a necessary part of the mortal experience. In mortality we would have ample opportunity to learn, grow, and prove ourselves by understanding God's laws and keeping His commandments.

Our loving Father promised that He would not leave us without guidance, alone and comfortless. We would not walk without assistance. To help us find our way, He would give us His word through the scriptures and inspired counsel from holy prophets. We could then choose to make life's decisions based on the Lord's plan rather than the worldly opinions of others.

In mortality we could also learn to seek personal revelation through fasting and prayer. As we grew and gained experience, we would learn to trust the promptings of the Holy Ghost. Our maturing spiritual instincts would tell us whether or not we were heading in the right direction. With the Holy Ghost as our guide, we could choose to follow righteous but narrow paths, less-traveled roads whose proximate twists and ultimate end would often be hidden from our limited mortal view.

God's design for us, immortality and eternal life, would be the destination. We would be free to choose this path of growth toward godhood.

There would be times when, try as hard as we could to obey the commandments and make the right choices for ourselves, we would experience the unwanted consequences of someone else's exercise of his or her own agency. The gift of agency and choice would of necessity cut both ways. Patient endurance would be an essential part of the celestial equation.

There was an alternative to the great plan of salvation. In the premortal existence, Lucifer proposed a fundamental modification of the Father's plan. It was a deceptively easier and more expedient concept. He, Lucifer himself, would predetermine the outcome and guarantee the results. But in so doing, he would destroy our agency and claim the glory and honor for his own.

Elder Dallin H. Oaks describes Satan's modification:

> He would save *all* the spirit children of God by eliminating the possibility of sin. He would assure that result by removing their power to choose (Moses 4:1, 3).
>
> Lucifer's modification could not be accepted because his proposed means were repugnant to the end sought to be achieved. In the world of ends and means, ends are inexorably shaped by the means used to achieve them. The objective of eternal life for the children of God could be attained only by the methods God would approve. As he has said in another setting: "It must needs be done in mine own way" (D&C 104:16).
>
> Lucifer's methods could not achieve God's objective. They would corrupt it. Saving everyone at the price of taking away everyone's agency would deny God's children the growth

toward eternal life they were intended to receive from the creation of the world and their venture into mortality.

—*The Lord's Way* (Salt Lake City: Deseret Book, 1991),
pp. viii–ix

The scriptures record that Satan's selfish proposal was rejected. As spirit children of God, those of us who subsequently came into mortality participated in rejecting that modification. Satan rebelled in anger and induced one-third of all the hosts of heaven to follow him.

For those who chose to follow Lucifer, the Father's "plan of happiness" was unacceptable. Perhaps the risk seemed too great and the way too difficult. They may have wanted an easier, safer path, the guaranteed results that were promised by Satan. The price might well have seemed deceptively small: loss of our power to choose.

But the power to choose—our moral agency—is absolutely essential to the plan of happiness and the further progression we must seek in mortality. With agency, we can learn, grow, improve, and progress. We are free to choose our own path. We can decide what we will do and who we will become.

The crucial importance of agency is reaffirmed again and again in the scriptures: "Wherefore, the Lord God gave unto man that he should act for himself" (2 Nephi 2:16); "Remember that ye are free to act for yourselves—to choose the way of everlasting death or the way of eternal life" (2 Nephi 10:23); "Behold, I gave unto him that he should be an agent unto himself" (D&C 29:35).

The Lord's servants have repeatedly reminded us that agency is a "sovereign principle. According to the plan [of salvation] agency must be honored. It was so from the beginning" (Boyd K. Packer, Conference Report, April 1988, p. 82). The scriptures indicate we probably have had our agency—and that God Himself honors and has vouchsafed it—at every stage of our existence:

> Man was also in the beginning with God. Intelligence, or the light of truth, was not created or made, neither indeed can be.
> All truth is independent in that sphere in which God has placed it, *to act for itself*, as all intelligence also; otherwise there is no existence.
> Behold, *here is the agency of man* . . .
> —D&C 93:29–31; italics added

The war in our premortal existence was fought over the issue of agency. As spirit children of God, we clearly had agency. We chose to follow the Father's plan, rejecting Satan's proposed modification that would have guaranteed the results but at the price of destroying our agency (Moses 4:3).

We also have our moral agency in mortality. The Lord said to Adam and Eve, "Thou mayest choose for thyself, for it is given unto thee" (Moses 3:17). To Enoch he said, "Behold these thy brethren; they are the workmanship of mine own hands, and I gave unto them their knowledge, in the day I created them; and *in the Garden of Eden, gave I unto man his agency*" (Moses 7:32; italics added).

In our own dispensation the Lord decreed, "Verily I say, men should be anxiously engaged in a good cause, and do many things of their own free will, and bring to pass much righteousness; for *the power is in them, wherein they are agents unto themselves*" (D&C 58:27–28; italics added).

For agency to be operative, there must be alternatives and opportunities from which to choose. As Lehi said, "It must needs be, that there is an opposition in all things." Good and evil. Light and darkness. Right and wrong. Easy and hard. (See 2 Nephi

27

2:11.) In Elder Holland's words, mortality presents us with the "chance to become like our heavenly parents, to face suffering and overcome it, to endure sorrow and still live rejoicingly, to confront good and evil and be strong enough to choose the good" (*Christ and the New Covenant,* p. 204).

Modern scriptures affirm the necessity of opposition: "It must needs be that the devil should tempt the children of men, or they could not be agents unto themselves" (D&C 29:39).

Thus we live in a world full of very real choices. Some are small. Others loom very large. All have consequences, both for ourselves and for others.

There is also a difference—and it is an essential one—between *agency* (the power to choose) and *freedom* (the opportunity to exercise those choices):

> Because *free agency* is a God-given precondition to the purpose of mortal life, no person or organization can take away our free agency in mortality . . . What can be taken away or reduced by the conditions of mortality is our *freedom,* the power to act upon our choices. Free agency is absolute, but in the circumstances of mortality freedom is always qualified.
>
> Freedom may be qualified or taken away by (1) physical laws, including the physical limitations with which we are born, (2) by our own action, and (3) by the action of others, including governments . . . A loss of freedom reduces the extent to which we can act upon our choices, but it does not deprive us of our God-given free agency . . .
>
> Many losses of freedom are imposed by others . . . Interferences with our freedom do not deprive us of our free agency. When Pharaoh put Joseph in prison, he restricted Joseph's freedom, but he did not take away his free agency.
>
> —Dallin H. Oaks, "Free Agency and Freedom,"
> address delivered at the Third Annual Book of

Laurel

President Howard W. Hunter said: "God's chief way of acting is by persuasion and patience and long-suffering, not by coercion and stark confrontation. He acts by gentle solicitation and by sweet enticement. *He always acts with unfailing respect for the freedom and independence that we possess*" (*Ensign*, November 1989, p. 18; italics added).

Other than the divine gift of life itself, the power to direct that life is God's most precious gift to us, His children. One of my favorite hymns, "Know This, That Every Soul Is Free," states:

> *Know this, that ev'ry soul is free*
> *To choose his life and what he'll be;*
> *For this eternal truth is giv'n:*
> *That God will force no man to heav'n.*
>
> *He'll call, persuade, direct aright,*
> *And bless with wisdom, love, and light,*
> *In nameless ways be good and kind,*
> *But never force the human mind.*
> —*Hymns,* no. 240

Unlike agency, our freedom—the opportunity together with the ability to exercise our agency—*can* be compromised. It may be restricted by others. It may be limited by circumstance. Our freedom can also be curtailed or willingly surrendered by our own choices and actions. We may even pursue one incorrect path for so long or repeat wrong behaviors so often that we lose the desire, the will, to change.

But agency itself cannot be surrendered or taken away. Agency is preserved under the most severe conditions, the most extreme circumstances. Even the extraordinarily degrading, dehumanizing surroundings exemplified by Hitler's concentration camps could not deprive captives of this most precious gift:

> The experiences of [concentration] camp life show that man does have a choice of action. . . . Man *can* preserve a vestige of spiritual freedom, of independence of mind, even in such terrible conditions of psychic and physical stress. . . .
>
> Everything can be taken from a man but one thing: the last of the human freedoms—to choose one's attitude in any given set of circumstances, to choose one's own way.
>
> There were always choices to make. Every day, every hour, offered the opportunity to make a decision, a decision which determined whether you would or would not submit to those powers which threatened to rob you of your very self, your inner freedom; which determined whether or not you would become the plaything of circumstance, renouncing freedom and dignity to become molded into the form of the typical inmate. . . . The last inner freedom cannot be lost.
>
> —Viktor Frankl, *Man's Search for Meaning* (New York: Simon & Schuster, 1984), pp. 74–75

It is this final internal liberty, our last inner stronghold, that cannot be usurped. Even in indescribably loathsome conditions, it remains to those of determined heart, undaunted will, and resolute spirit. We cannot always control our circumstances, but we can determine how we respond to them.

In LDS theology, "impaired agency" is thus an oxymoron. "Impaired will" is not.

Both external and internal threats to our freedom exist in abundance. There are numerous influences around us that will—if we allow them to do so—sap our spiritual strength, dissolve our determination, and erode our will to choose our own paths, to elect our own way.

We must never, ever willingly surrender or relinquish our freedom to direct our own lives. In so doing, we may figuratively sell the opportunity to exercise agency, our precious celestial birthright, for a mess of temporal pottage. To whatever extent possible, we should resist those circumstances that would restrict or limit our freedom to choose for ourselves. We should permit no one and *no thing* to usurp our freedom to make moral choices.

There are also, especially today, some substances and behavior patterns that can be frighteningly effective solvents of our will to resist evil. Those who surrender themselves to their pernicious influence may be plunged into a spiritual Twilight Zone from which escape can be very difficult . . .

Chapter 4

Pottage and Other Messes

The call came, as they so often do, at the end of a particularly long, hard day at the hospital. I had already packed my briefcase, put my coat on, and started toward the door of my office when the phone rang. One of my favorite colleagues, a local neurologist practicing in Salt Lake City, was waiting on the line.

"Annie," he said in a hopeful but anxious tone, "you going to be around for a while?"

I knew that innocent-sounding question really meant he had something serious on his mind. He needed to talk—now.

"As a matter of fact, I was planning to stay late and work on some stuff in my office," I said, mentally excusing the small white lie.

His relief was evident. "Good!" he exclaimed. "I've got a tough case I'd like to show you. I've got all the films here and I could run right up to your office. Be there in ten minutes!"

"I'll leave the door open," I replied, resigned to the delay.

He hurried in a few minutes later, slightly out of breath. I pulled out a chair for him and turned on a bank of x-ray viewboxes so we could look at the films together.

He wasted no time in getting to the point. "One of my patients, a young mother of two whom I've been seeing off and on

33

for chronic headaches, was admitted to the hospital the day before yesterday with strokelike symptoms and elevated blood pressure. The initial CAT scan was negative so we did an MRI," he said, referring to another kind of medical imaging called magnetic resonance imaging.

Working while he talked, he placed the CAT scan on the viewbox. I glanced at it briefly and agreed that it looked normal. The neurologist took it down and put a half-dozen MRI films on the illuminated panels.

"This is what has us concerned," he remarked worriedly as he pointed to several abnormal areas on the brain scan. "We don't know what's going on here."

"Is she pregnant?" I asked.

"No."

"On birth control pills? Or any other medications?"

"No."

"Is there any history of recent infection? Possible trauma or other kind of injury?"

"No," he said again with obvious frustration.

"Hmpf," I grunted as I looked at the films in more detail. "These changes could represent emboli from the heart. Or perhaps some sort of abnormality in the distal blood vessels, a vasculitis of some kind. Maybe even lupus."

"That's what we thought," he agreed. "But her cardiac examination is normal. So far all the laboratory studies are negative, too. We were stumped, so I asked the neuroradiologists to do an angiogram."

"Sounds reasonable," I agreed. "Have they done it yet?"

"Just finished it this afternoon. I brought all those films, too."

I had suspected as much, judging from the bulky film jacket

he had with him. I sighed inwardly, knowing that sorting through the lengthy study was going to take time and careful attention.

"Well, let's start putting 'em up," I said, reaching for the heavy pile of films.

The very first images began to tell a fascinating but ominous story. I involuntarily sucked in my breath as striking abnormalities were apparent on one film after another.

"Wow!" I exclaimed, and it was an understatement. "I don't think I've ever personally seen anything quite like this!"

"Neither had we," he admitted. "We all hoped you'd know what was going on. We don't have a clue!"

"I do have some ideas," I mused as I searched through the remaining pile.

He looked hopeful.

"What about the sed rate? Is it elevated? Did you screen for anti-nuclear antibodies?" I asked, considering the possibility of diseases that involved malfunctions in the immune system. The body normally follows a sort of biological "behavioral code," leaving healthy cells alone while attacking cancers and harmful substances such as microbes and toxins. When autoimmune responses go awry, the body can figuratively "mutiny" and attack itself.

"Sed rate is within normal limits. But a lot of the other stuff is still cooking," he answered, referring to some still-pending blood studies.

"What about AIDS? It's comparatively rare in our neck of the woods but it *can* cause a vasculitis," I reminded him.

"Naw. We did test for HIV anyway. Negative."

Reluctantly, I raised another possibility. I hated to consider it, but I felt the issue had to be addressed. "What about drug abuse?"

He chuckled equably and answered, "No way. We're talking

active members of the Church here. This is a tithe-paying, temple-going, model Latter-day Saint couple. They're both school-teachers."

"Just thought I'd ask. Maybe you should too. As unlikely as it seems," I added hastily.

"They'd be insulted. If they got mad enough, they might even sue," he shuddered.

"I still think you should consider broaching the subject. Especially if all the other labs come back negative," I responded stubbornly.

"Easy for you to say," he muttered. "You don't have to talk to the patients."

I shrugged, out of ideas. We parted with a few pleasantries and a handshake.

A few weeks later, I saw my neurologist friend at a local medical conference.

"Hey," I called to him, "I haven't seen you for a few days."
We exchanged greetings.

"Oh, by the way," I asked casually, "whatever came of that case you showed me a couple of weeks ago? How did it turn out? I'd be interested to know what the final diagnosis was."

He looked a bit embarrassed.

"I took your advice," he said with a rueful grin. "I felt uneasy about that case all along. Something just didn't fit. After we finished at your office, it was really nagging at me. So I went back to the hospital. Both the husband and wife were there. I closed the door and said, 'Sit down. We've got to talk.'"

He continued, "They both looked wary. I decided to take the bull by the horns and just asked bluntly, 'Do you use drugs?' They were outraged, indignant that I'd even dare ask such a thing. They vehemently denied it. Threatened. The madder they got, the more certain I was that something was very wrong."

His shoulders slumped. "It took a long time, but I kept after them. Then it finally came out. Cocaine. And maybe some other stuff as well."

It fit. The whole puzzling case now made logical but tragic sense.

"You know what they said, when they finally admitted to using coke?" he asked. "I could hardly believe my ears. 'We're not addicts,' they said. 'We're not like others,' they said. 'We don't do it very often,' they said. 'Couple times a week, max.' Then the capper, the absolute top: 'We're *responsible users!*'"

"Ridiculous. There is no such thing as a 'responsible user' when you're talking about street drugs or abuse of prescription drugs," I stated flatly.

"Yeah," he concurred with a weary shrug, "and it happens even here. Right here in our own blessed valley."

I'm in control? I'm a "responsible user"? Rubbish! Rationalization and evasion are part of the addiction syndrome.

The road to addiction is a deceptive one. The beginning is not often clearly defined. There are no bold signposts that announce its inception, no well-demarcated boundaries that mark its stages. What is the difference between personal preferences, habits, and rituals on the one hand and frank dependence and addiction on the other? When does a habit become an addiction?

For that matter, how does curiosity become fascination, then grow into intense interest and preoccupation, perhaps eventually becoming fixation and even compulsion?

In society's version of diagnostic "bracket creep," such distinctions as these are often ignored, deliberately blurred, or even eliminated. *Addiction* has a nasty, judgmental sound, some might say. But I would argue in response that addiction is a truly nasty and uniquely destructive business.

There are many different types of addictions. Some are chemical; some are psychological; some are behavioral. Some represent a combination of several factors. Eating disorders. Alcohol abuse. Pornography. Sexual addiction. Drug abuse (involving both illicit "street" and prescription drugs).

Not all addictions are alike, but there are some common threads that they seem to share. Misery is one. Pleasure-seeking is sometimes another. There is often a strongly felt need to escape stress and relieve pain, whether physical, psychological, or a mixture of both.

The welcome relief or transient pleasure derived from using an addictive substance soon dissipates, leaving in its wake a desire, a hunger, even a craving for more. In a very real phenomenon medical doctors call "tachyphylaxis," the body and the brain develop a tolerance to certain substances. This results in the body's requiring ever-increasing amounts of the drug—painkillers, for example—to achieve the desired effect such as pleasure or relief from pain.

A similar kind of adaptation can take place with behavioral addictions. For example, addiction to pornography may demand ever more bizarre and explicit material to satisfy the need. Eventually, viewing the material—no matter how extreme—may not be enough.

Regarding the devil's goal of twisting, exaggerating, and perverting normal human pleasure to his own end, C. S. Lewis wrote, "An ever increasing craving for an ever diminishing pleasure is the formula . . . to get the man's soul and give him *nothing* in return" (*The Screwtape Letters* [New York: Bantam, 1995], p. 26).

I believe that addiction—of any kind, to any thing—is one of the greatest potential threats to our freedom. There are some potent substances such as cocaine, heroin, and certain "designer drugs" whose effect on the brain is so powerful that, at least in some people, they can be almost instantaneously addicting.

Jonathan Kellerman, a psychologist and author of numerous popular suspense novels, recently wrote about his own personal encounter with what he called a "chemically induced thrill system." In the first pain-wracked hours after cancer surgery, he was given a narcotic similar to morphine. He describes vividly how the drug transported him from total body pain and agony to euphoria and blessed relief, then—as it wore off—slammed him back into "post-op hell."

After dramatically describing the drug-crave curve, Dr. Kellerman concluded: "Any substance capable of transporting a psyche from agony to rapture that powerfully and quickly is beyond empathy and rationality. Morphiates stimulate a level of pleasure incomprehensible to those who haven't experienced it."

The mere thought of experimenting with such potent substances personally scares the daylights out of me. It terrified Dr. Kellerman too. As a counselor and psychologist, he knew firsthand the devastating ruins created by drug abuse. After his initial experience of flying high on medical heroin, he opted instead for a single dose of oral Percoset, then eventually downshifted to Tylenol for the remainder of his hospitalization. As he put it, "The pain wasn't nice but it ended" (*USA Today*, 9 June 1997, p. 19A).

This reminds me of a chilling discussion I had a few years ago with some medical colleagues. We were discussing the tragic death of Len Bias, a highly talented young athlete who had just been drafted into the NBA by the Boston Celtics. Instant fame, numerous lucrative product endorsements, and a multimillion-dollar contract surely awaited him.

The promising young man, who had no known history of drug abuse, tried cocaine. Apparently he used it just once. The drug, which can hit the brain and cardiovascular system like a sledgehammer, caused a fatal heart attack.

We asked ourselves why someone would throw away such a bright future. How could anybody be that naive? Did he feel invulnerable? Did he think nothing would happen to him? No one knew the answers. None of us understood the drug's allure and power.

As we were all shaking our heads, one of the young doctors asked me bluntly, "Annie, have you ever tried it?"

"What's 'it'?" I asked.

"Coke."

"No."

"Marijuana?"

"Nope."

"Not even once? Maybe way back when you were in college, in the heyday of the counterculture movement? Maybe you tried it but just 'didn't inhale'?"

"No, never."

"What's the matter, don't you trust yourself?" he challenged. "Afraid? Think you might not be strong-willed enough to keep it under control?"

"That's absolutely right," I answered emphatically. "The whole idea scares me. I simply don't want to take the risk—either of a drug reaction or of becoming addicted. The first use could be the last one, as it was for Len Bias. In fact, where drugs are concerned, I *don't* trust myself—or anyone else either. So, no, I'm not at all sure I'd be 'strong enough,' at least the way you seem to be defining strength. I'd rather be strong enough never to try the dog-goned stuff in the first place!"

There are wide variations in individual susceptibility to both illegal and legal drugs like alcohol and tobacco. I'd rather not test the limits of my own resistance to such substances. Better to stay as far away from the cliff's edge as possible and avoid looking curiously into the abyss beyond. Cliff walking is a hazardous occupation; vertigo and loss of balance are real risks when you get so close to the edge.

President Gordon B. Hinckley has pleaded with us, every one of us, to shun illegal drugs as we would avoid poison. I'll bet he's never tried them either—the very thought seems patently ridiculous, doesn't it?

The "if you haven't tried it, don't knock it" school of thought doesn't apply to using illegal drugs or abusing prescription drugs. This is clearly such a terribly dangerous path that we should never even put a foot on it. Not so much as a toenail!

When and how does a person cross the vanishingly thin line into dependence and addiction? It's not always clear. But one thing I know for certain is this: We have one definite, well-defined, absolutely crystal clear choice, and it is the very first one. For some people and certain substances, it may in fact be the only one.

That choice: Don't even try drugs! Avoid them like the very plague on our society that they are. They may well destroy you and all you hold dear. There is no such thing as a "responsible user."

Speaking of substance abuse, the director of Stanford University's Alcohol and Drug Treatment Center wrote, "The person in the grips of dependence does not have biological control." He emphasized further, "In classic withdrawal, the abuser loses control over his central nervous system response to the psychoactive substance" (in "Dependence Diagnosed," *Stanford Medicine,* Fall 1996, pp. 8–9).

President Hinckley recently instructed priesthood leaders, "Let us work with our children, teach our people, to not become shackled and enslaved by drugs which take possession until the individual no longer has power over himself and cannot control his own destiny" (*Church News,* 6 July 1996).

Other servants of the Lord have been no less emphatic. Elder Robert D. Hales has firmly stated, "The use of alcohol, tobacco, and drugs should turn on warning lights because, when we choose to use these substances, *we become slaves; our agency is limited*" (Conference Report, April 1990, p. 53; italics added). And Elder Dallin H. Oaks has counseled: "We should avoid any practices in which one person attempts to surrender even part of his will to another person or in which another person attempts to take it. *Whether the means are chemical, behavioral, electronic, or others not yet dreamed of . . .* we should avoid *any* behavior that is addictive. *Whatever is addictive compromises our will*" ("Free Agency and Freedom," italics added).

Although addiction may severely weaken an individual's will and its consequences greatly restrict his freedom, his agency remains intact. The divine gift still flickers in the darkness. Elder Boyd K. Packer said, "It is contrary to the order of heaven for any soul to be locked into compulsive, immoral behavior with no way out" (*Ensign,* November 1986, p. 18). Thus the person in the grips of dependence who has surrendered his or her will to addictive behavior still has one final remaining freedom, one last desperate choice: the choice to cry for help.

All is not yet lost. If recognized, addiction can be assessed and treated effectively. The road is, admittedly, very difficult. Treatment failures are common and relapses are discouragingly frequent. The good news is that recovery is possible; dependence can be conquered and addiction can be overcome.

If you are suffering with addiction, do not despair. There is hope for those who feel hopeless.

Loving, genuinely concerned Church leaders and experienced professional counselors are available to assist you in finding the path back. It is a difficult, thorny, and taxing road that lies ahead. In some cases it will require a lifetime of unrelentingly hard work and all the help you can get to escape from the iron grasp of dependency and addiction.

But, after all, an eternity hangs in the balance.

God can give us strength and power beyond our own to overcome all things. Addiction is no exception.

Chapter 5

High Noon in the Garden
of Good and Evil

The visual image is compelling, even arresting. It's a common story line, the stuff of oft-told modern tales as well as the basis for ancient legends. It's the classic theme of countless novels and a popular script for Western movies.

The sheriff walks slowly but with steady, measured gait down the dusty main street of a rough-and-tumble town on the American frontier. It is high noon in the Old West, time to face the Bad Guys. The hero is virtuous, with rugged good looks, firm jaw, and steely, determined eyes.

The odds against him are usually overwhelming. He almost always walks alone. Unafraid.

You know who the Bad Guys are; they wear the black hats.

In another movie theater halfway around the world, the same scene is played out by a samurai warrior with his long and short swords, the *katana* and *tanto,* tucked precisely into his wide *obi* sash. He dresses neatly, usually wearing an immaculate blue or gray kimono. He is clean-cut and handsome. The samurai typically walks alone, this time to face the rogues and bullies who have been terrorizing the poor village. He strides proudly, filled with a

45

deep abiding sense of *giri* or obligation. To him, honor and loyalty are the supreme virtues.

A visual shorthand quickly tells the rapt audience who the Bad Guys are: they are homely, with messy, unkempt hair; they are clad in ugly black kimonos. Sometimes an eye patch is added to complete the sinister look.

Here at home, in the valleys and high mountains of Utah, at first glance the Good Guy appears much less imposing, perhaps even ordinary. He is slight in physical stature and much older than the prototype hero. He too has faced long odds, walking less-traveled roads in his tireless efforts to choose the right and entreat others to do the same. Because he loves people and wants to be among them, he is rarely alone.

He carries no guns, wears no swords. His armor is not the visible kind.

It is high noon. But he's been there before. Many times.

There are no Bad Guys, at least not the easily identifiable kind. Immorality doesn't always wear a black hat. Sleaze isn't necessarily dressed in a dirty kimono.

The Good Guy often functions with an additional handicap in the never-ending struggle with wrong. There are always curious onlookers and sometimes even a few hecklers who would distract his attention and try to spoil his uncompromising aim at evil. Instead of pistols and knives, those detractors use words. Cameras. Notepads and recorders. They know better than to try a frontal attack, for his ready wit, gentle good humor, infectious optimism, and legendary warmth will disarm even the most determined opponent. They will probe for any weakness, ready to move quickly and exploit any opening. They will be disappointed.

His demeanor is one of quiet confidence. He appears calm and assured, but there is not one iota of arrogance or egoism in the man. If anything, his deep-seated humility augments his widespread appeal.

He commands no troops, heads no warrior legions. Yet his power and authority are incalculable. His is a moral leadership, derived from personal righteousness, unimpeachable integrity, and his divinely constituted office. He has been tried in the fires of affliction and has not been found wanting.

He is Gordon Bitner Hinckley, fifteenth President of The Church of Jesus Christ of Latter-day Saints. His people, of whom I am one, revere him as a prophet, the latest in a long, distinguished line that includes Joseph Smith and Brigham Young in this modern dispensation and stretches back in time to Moses, Enoch, Abraham, Isaac, and Jacob. Yes, Amulek and Alma, along with Lehi and Nephi, are among those both honored and burdened with the prophetic calling.

President Hinckley never browbeats, never harangues. He inspires and quietly encourages his attentive listeners with simple, soft-spoken phrases. By nature a modest man, he characteristically includes himself in his admonitions. With a smile that brings him close to his audience he remarks, "We can all do a little better." He makes people *want* to be better. Feeling his trust in their basic goodness and decency, they believe they really *can* be better.

He exudes hope and an invigorating spirit of optimism. "What a great future there is for you if you will just walk the right way," he often says. "You are wonderful and you have within you the potential to do great and marvelous and good things. . . . Don't get sidetracked. Do what is right, let the consequence follow" (*Church News,* 6 May 1997). He has boundless confidence in us! When we hear such words of encouragement we feel a surge of energy and determination. We *know* we can do it.

President Hinckley also knows and often teaches that it is

rarely the big choices in our lives that destroy us. He stresses that small, seemingly unimportant decisions can be pivotal: "The little decisions can be so crucial and so everlastingly important in their consequences" (Conference Report, October 1994, p. 65). It is these small and simple things, the daily little choices we make that largely determine our course.

Of such small choices are lives made. And unmade.

Chapter 6

A Name and Face for Evil

He has many names and various guises. Some are as old as history itself; others are more modern inventions. His generic title in almost every language translates as "the devil." The ancient Hebrews first knew him as a member of the heavenly court who functioned as "the accuser," an agent of opposition and obstruction. He was later characterized as the great Other in a perpetual cosmic war between good and evil.

Common appellations for the devil have included Satan, Lucifer, Mephistopheles, and even "Old Scratch." He has been variously called the prince of darkness, the great imitator, the master deceiver, the father of lies. In the lyrics of a song by a popular hard rock group, the Rolling Stones, the devil was even misleadingly described as "a man of wealth and taste."

Terms such as *evil, the devil, sin* and *repentance* are becoming increasingly rare in modern conversation. They are deemed by many as dogmatic, much too judgmental, and far too harsh for proper discourse in polite circles. Many seem to think that unenlightened individuals who stubbornly persist in their antiquated belief in evil and the devil are to be pitied. Those who dare believe evil actually has a name and a face are dismissed as superstitious at best, even mentally somewhat off-kilter.

In his preface to *The Screwtape Letters,* C. S. Lewis wrote: "There are two equal and opposite errors into which our race can fall about the devils. One is to disbelieve in their existence. The other is to believe, and to feel an excessive and unhealthy interest in them." As he also advised his readers to remember, "The safest road to Hell is the gradual one—the gentle slope, soft underfoot, without sudden turnings, without milestones, without signposts."

More than a century ago, the French poet Baudelaire cautioned, "Never forget . . . that the Devil's cleverest ploy is to persuade you that he doesn't exist." Could Baudelaire have borrowed an idea from the Book of Mormon? His statement sounds very much like Nephi's warning concerning the devil's activities in our own day and age:

> For behold, at that day shall he rage in the hearts of the children of men, and stir them up to anger against that which is good.
>
> And others will he pacify, and lull them away into carnal security, that they will say: All is well in Zion; yea, Zion prospereth, all is well—and thus the devil cheateth their souls, and leadeth them away carefully down to hell.
>
> And behold, others he flattereth away, and telleth them there is no hell; and he saith unto them: I am no devil, for there is none—and thus he whispereth in their ears, until he grasps them with his awful chains, from whence there is no deliverance.
>
> —2 Nephi 28:20–22

As Nephi foresaw, today Satan gets the silent treatment from the media while evil is erased from our attention and expunged from our conversational vocabulary. Reporting on a recent Christian Booksellers Convention, a 1995 *Newsweek* article noted that under "S" the list of available publications included hundreds of titles for "success" and "seasonal" but almost none for "Satan" and "sin." One wonders what they would have found under "E" ... probably not "evil."

In his novel *The Witches of Eastwick,* John Updike has one of the witches demur, "Evil is not a word we like to use. We prefer to say 'unfortunate' or 'lacking' or 'misguided' or 'disadvantaged.' We prefer to think of evil as the absence of good, a momentary relenting of its sunshine, a shadow, a weakening" (New York: Random House, 1984).

We are also watching the unnaming of Satan and the elimination of evil as objective reality in Western religious tradition. To many mainstream Christian theologians, evil itself is not only unfashionable, it is illusory. It doesn't really exist. Evil is, in classic Augustinian tradition, regarded only as the absence of good. Thus evil is literally nothing. As a mere "privation of the good," evil has only a "negative reality."

Let us not demean those who died in Bosnia or suffered from Stalin, Mao, Hitler, and Pol Pot with such nonsense.

To its victims, evil is real. Contrary to one historian's famous assertion about the "banality of evil," to its sufferers evil is *never* commonplace.

Evil as "negative reality"? Satan as mere metaphor? Nothing could be further from the truth.

Andrew Delbanco, chronicling the deconstruction of the devil in *The Death of Satan: How Americans Have Lost the Sense of Evil,* remarked with wonder, "The work of the devil is everywhere, but no one knows where to find him. We live in the most brutal century in human history, but instead of stepping forward to take the credit, he has rendered himself invisible" (New York: Farrar, Straus and Giroux, 1995, p. 9).

The devil has done a mighty slick disappearing act.

Evil is real. I firmly believe Satan exists. He is no abstraction, no mere absence of the good. Neither is he a nebulous manifestation like the "dark side of the Force" in the popular Star Wars trilogy.

Satan is by no means a far-off, remote figure. He is, by contrast, a familiar if not ubiquitous personage. President Spencer W. Kimball described him as "very much a personal, individual spirit being, but without a mortal body. . . . Yes, the devil is decidedly a person" (*The Miracle of Forgiveness* [Salt Lake City: Bookcraft, 1969], p. 21).

At one time or another, many people have at least felt his influence and heard his whisperings of enticement. Calling Satan the master deceiver and reminding us that it is important to know and recognize his methods, President James E. Faust has asked: "Who has not heard and felt the enticings of the devil? His voice often sounds so reasonable and his message so easy to justify. It is an enticing, intriguing voice with dulcet tones. . . . The prince of darkness can be found everywhere . . . his influence is everywhere."

President Faust went on to state: "The First Presidency described Satan: 'He is working under such perfect disguise that many do not recognize either him or his methods. There is no crime he would not commit, no debauchery he would not set up, no plague he would not send, no heart he would not break, no life he would not take, no soul he would not destroy. He comes as a thief in the night; he is a wolf in sheep's clothing' (James R. Clark, comp., *Messages of the First Presidency of The Church of Jesus Christ of Latter-day Saints*, 6 vols., Salt Lake City: Bookcraft, 1965–1975, 6:179)." (*Ensign*, November 1987, pp. 33–36).

I don't have any Satan stories to relate. I've never personally stared into the eyes of evil, nor have I taken Satan on in a head-to-head, toe-to-toe spiritual wrestling match. I hope I never do. No good can possibly come from getting too close to evil. We must avoid the devil's territory of temptation and deceit like the plague it is, has always been, and forever will be.

Still, it is essential to know our ancient enemy and understand his methods so that we will recognize his works for what they are. Brigham Young said it is important to "study evil, and its consequences" (*Discourses of Brigham Young,* comp. John A. Widtsoe [Salt Lake City: Deseret Book, 1941], p. 257). However, I believe it is far safer to learn about evil indirectly and at as great a distance as possible. Instead of seeking our own personal encounters with Satan, we can easily—and certainly much more safely—learn about him and his methods through studying the scriptures.

The Savior Himself had a very revealing dialogue with the devil following his forty-day fast in the wilderness. Satan's bold presumption and arrogance with Him who created worlds without number—including our own—is nothing short of astonishing (see Matthew 4:1–11; Luke 4:1–13).

As a fourteen-year-old boy, Joseph Smith knelt in a secluded wood near his home, praying fervently to the Lord for truth and light. Almost immediately he found himself surrounded by thick darkness and sinking into deep despair. For a time it even seemed as if he were doomed to destruction. He later wrote that he was nearly overcome by "the power of some actual being from the unseen world," and described its influence as "such marvelous power as I had never before felt in any being" (Joseph Smith–History 1:15–16).

The Prophet explained that he then exerted all his powers to call upon God and deliver him from the enemy who had seized him. At the very moment when he was ready to sink into despair and abandon himself to destruction, God the Father and His Only Begotten Son, Jesus Christ, appeared to the young boy and delivered him from the adversary's awful grasp. This glorious First Vision opened the dispensation of the fulness of times.

We can only surmise what actually happened, but we can assume that the adversary probably would have known the significance of what was about to transpire. He surely knew of Joseph's foreordination as the first prophet of the last, great dispensation. He would also have known that Joseph would prove a most effective disturber and annoyer of his kingdom. Had Satan succeeded in his efforts to prevent the First Vision from taking place, the course of history and the future of millions of souls would have been dramatically altered.

One of the many fundamental and important lessons of the First Vision is that Satan exists. His power is very real. However, as the Prophet learned and later taught, "All beings who have bodies have power over those who have not. The devil has no power over us only as we permit him" (*Teachings of the Prophet Joseph Smith,* sel. Joseph Fielding Smith [Salt Lake City: Deseret Book, 1976], p. 181).

Joseph Smith experienced firsthand the reality and power of Satan.

I'll take his word for it.

President Marion G. Romney wrote, "Latter-day Saints know that there is a God. With like certainty, they know that Satan lives, that he is a powerful personage of spirit, the archenemy of God, of man, and of righteousness" (*Ensign,* June 1971, p. 35). Elder Neal A. Maxwell likewise said, "One cannot believe in the living God whom the living scriptures describe and who is spoken about by living prophets, and still not come to understand too that there is also a devil" (*Things As They Really Are* [Salt Lake City: Deseret Book, 1980], p. 40).

Even when they grudgingly grant the independent existence of evil, modern commentators caricature Satan and minimize the magnitude of his influence. One writer said, "Today, evil is experienced as random and ordinary, devoid of cosmic significance. '– – – – [expletive deleted] happens,' we say with a shrug."

As a college student from a traditional Protestant background, I struggled with the "problem" of evil. If, as I believed, God created everything from nothing (the classic *ex nihilo* concept of orthodox Christianity), where did evil come from? As the Creator, isn't God at least indirectly responsible for evil? If so, how could a good, loving God create evil?

In Mormon theology, the evil that men do and the suffering they cause in their own lives and the lives of others are the inevitable by-products of genuine moral agency. Given the power to choose, some will elect to choose evil.

President Gordon B. Hinckley has reminded us:

> There is another war that has gone on since before the world was created and which is likely to continue for a long time yet to come. . . . That war has never ceased.
>
> The war goes on. It is waged across the world over the issues of agency and compulsion. It is waged in our own lives, day in and day out, in our homes, in our work, in our school associations; it is waged over questions of love and respect, of loyalty and fidelity, of obedience and integrity. We are all involved in it . . . each one of us.
>
> —*Church News,* 8 February 1997

This is no abstract and impersonal battle, no remote, imaginary conflict. Although it is a cosmic struggle, this ongoing war is fought well within our view, inside the boundaries of our own lives, indeed, very close to home. Sometimes it is actually *in* the home. At other times it is on our streets or within our workplaces.

Satan is an intimate enemy. We are all locked into the eternal universal struggle between the constructive, elevating, and positive forces of good and the destructive, debasing, and negative influence of evil.

There is indeed "a line drawn in the sand."

We will, by our actions—or even our failure to act—choose one side of that line or the other. Each of us makes choices between good and evil, between right and wrong, several times a day. With countless small but significant decisions, we determine our course. We must select our path firmly and courageously. We must be steadfast and unwavering in our determination to choose the right and resist the wrong. As one verse from the hymn "The Time Is Far Spent" puts it:

> *Be fixed in your purpose, for Satan will try you;*
> *The weight of your calling he perfectly knows.*
> *Your path may be thorny, but Jesus is nigh you;*
> *His arm is sufficient, tho demons oppose.*
> —Hymns, no. 266

The opposition is often alluring, its audacity intimidating, its methods seductive. The sheer scale of modern evil is also shocking and appalling. In the words of Andrew Delbanco, "The repertoire of evil has never been richer." Yet President Gordon B. Hinckley's assessment of the ongoing battle is characteristically upbeat and optimistic: "We are winning, and the future never looked brighter."

We all have a moral mandate to name evil and oppose its influence. Anywhere. Everywhere. Anytime. All the time.

For every last one of us, today is indeed high noon in the garden of good and evil.

FOLLOWING THE ROAD
Choosing the Less-Traveled Way

"I was called and I would not hear . . . I knew, yet I would not know," Amulek tells us (see Alma 10:6). Nevertheless, at the pivotal decision point of his life, Amulek made the right choice.

When we know that choosing one path means abandoning another, perhaps more familiar or comfortable road, we may also be tempted to "not hear," to stick with the easier way. Yet, like Amulek, deep down inside we often sense that the harder, more obscure road is indeed the right one.

Chapter 7

Less-Traveled Roads

We never noticed the searing summer heat and suffocating humidity. Children rarely do. To us, the hot Indiana summers were a magical time of year.

We were fortunate, living relatively near a lake. Our property was not actually *on* the water, mind you; that prime real estate was occupied by an exclusive, private preparatory school and expensive weekend homes owned mostly by wealthy out-of-towners. The majority of us "locals" lived on adjacent farms or in the small town that bordered the less desirable part of the lake.

The swampy northwest corner was also home to the town park and its popular public beach and boat launch. A weedy section of the lakefront was reserved as an anchorage for the modest craft and fishing boats owned by a few of the luckier locals. Dad and my Uncle Bob shared a pier where the Osborn "fleet" was moored every year. It consisted of our grandfather's old aluminum rowboat, a small, sloop-rigged sailboat called a "Snipe," and—our pride and joy—a sturdy, clinker-built ski boat with a big Johnson outboard motor and twin five-gallon metal gas tanks.

Law and order on the lake was maintained mostly by common courtesy. There were relatively few misdemeanors; violent crime was almost unknown.

The only officer was a popular junior high school coach cum history teacher who was hired part-time for the summer by the Lake Association and deputized by the local two-man police force. He was fortyish, a ruggedly handsome man with a hook nose, flat-top haircut, and piercing, gray-blue eyes. He took both his jobs—teacher and law officer—equally seriously.

Jim Cox—*Mister* Cox, if you please—could intimidate his students with a single stern glance.

The boaters were a different story.

As the lake traffic increased each summer and the speedboats became more powerful, it finally became apparent that the modest patrol boat the Lake Association had used for years would no longer suffice.

The Town Fathers and the Lake Association leaders bit the bullet, pooled their resources, and purchased a craft that would be by far the fastest boat on the lake. It was a top-of-the-line model, an inboard with a powerful engine designed for speed.

The boat was painted a brilliant white with "Lake Patrol" emblazoned in bold letters on its sharply raked bow. It was magnificent. When Mr. Cox opened the throttle wide, the boat went so fast it almost seemed to be hydroplaning. The sleek new craft was the talk of the lake.

There was only one minor problem. The neat but well-worn uniforms the Association provided hardly matched the dazzling boat's splendor.

So sorry, the Town Fathers and Lake Association officers replied to Mr. Cox's pleas for new uniforms. *We spent the whole budget on the boat.* They apologized with a vague promise. *Perhaps next year . . .*

Undeterred, Mr. Cox asked permission to buy his own uniforms. Despite their puzzlement at why anyone would want to spend his own hard-earned money unnecessarily, they reluctantly gave him the go-ahead.

The next weekend, Mr. Cox went on patrol decked out in his brand-new duds. He had made a special trip to South Bend, the nearest big city, and spent several hours in a uniform store, painstakingly selecting each item for maximum effect. The resulting outfit made him look something like a cross between an Indiana state trooper and a Canadian mountie.

He wore a crisp, short-sleeved khaki shirt tucked into precisely tailored pants that were pressed into knife-edge creases. A Sam Browne belt crossed his muscular chest under shoulder epaulets and attached to a wide matching tan leather belt. His sidearm, a .38 pistol, was carefully holstered on his hip along with the usual assortment of billy club and handcuffs (never used), army knife, and screwdriver and pliers (often used). The latter tools were employed for impromptu repairs on the stalled engines of hapless boaters who found themselves adrift, bobbing helplessly in the middle of the lake.

Mr. Cox's silver deputy's badge was polished to a fare-thee-well and glinted brightly in the summer sunshine. Opaque, aviator-style, wrap-around sunglasses added to the overall effect. Best of all, the whole outfit was topped off by a broad-brimmed, high-crowned, brown felt hat with chinstrap—the eye-catching kind that Smokey the Bear ("Help Prevent Forest Fires") wore on television.

Mr. Cox cut a splendid figure and he knew it.

He proudly drove the Lake Patrol boat up and down the entire three-mile length of the lake, cheerily waving at bathers and wary boaters.

We were often on the lake, as waterskiing was one of our family's favorite activities. We would slalom for hours, cutting sharply and jumping back and forth across the waves, competing with

61

other boats to see whose skiiers could throw up the biggest rooster tails of water. Extra points were awarded informally for taking an especially spectacular spill or touching a shoulder to the water without falling.

The only problem with a day of sun and skiing (skin cancer wouldn't become an issue until years in the future) was that the tanks in our boat didn't hold very much gas. Once or twice a day, we would have to motor to the lake's only marina and fill 'em up.

We loved Campbell's marina. It occupied a small, stagnant lagoon on the south end of the lake and was ringed by boat houses, commercial docks, and warehouses adjoined by a large boatyard. The place smelled of oil, suntan lotion, engine exhaust and rotting vegetation. It was the scent of summer.

Late one memorable holiday weekend we detoured into the marina to fill up and grab a quick bite to eat. We chatted on the dock as one of the local boys who worked at the marina topped off the tanks for us.

As we stood there, the Lake Patrol boat hove into view, smartly rounding the corner into the lagoon. Mr. Cox, hat cocked at a rakish angle, expertly maneuvered it into a miniscule slot adjacent to the gas pumps. He tossed the bowline to a waiting attendant and gestured for a fill-up.

Then the unthinkable happened. When Mr. Cox stepped onto the gunwale of the boat and put his other foot on the dock, he failed to transfer his weight properly. His legs spread-eagled as the boat began to push away from the dock.

Oddly, no one moved. The suddenly hushed crowd on the dock stood in a frozen tableau, mouths agape, as the inevitable result soon became apparent.

"Aw, hell!" he exclaimed in disgust just before he at last lost his balance and fell into the oily water with a resounding *ker-plunk*.

For a moment, all that the onlookers could see was his Smokey-the-Bear hat slowly floating away toward the center of the lagoon.

Then he surfaced, coughing and spluttering indignantly.

The spell broke as the crowd erupted into laughter. One of the boys dived into the water and retrieved the beloved hat as others reached down and hoisted the sopping wet policeman onto the dock.

"It's not funny!" he shouted, removing his gun and pouring scummy water out of the dripping holster. Then, realizing how ridiculous he must look, he began chuckling along with everyone else.

The boy carefully brushed water and seaweed off the hat and solemnly handed it back to Mr. Cox.

With a broad grin he clapped it onto his head, readjusted the brim to its customary jaunty angle, and drove off toward the setting sun. There were other boats to be hailed and—hopefully—a few more tickets yet to be written before night fell.

Years later, I can still visualize poor Mr. Cox struggling to maintain his balance with one foot on the boat's gunwale and the other on the dock.

How often do *we*, in indecision, try to straddle between the world and the Lord's kingdom? It's a dangerous balancing act, one in which nonchoice becomes a choice. The result may be a spiritual fall into murky water.

Joshua warned the Israelites, "Choose you this day whom ye will serve," and concluded with his own decision, "As for me and my house, we will serve the Lord" (Joshua 24:15).

The Prophet Elijah pleaded, "How long halt ye between two opinions? If the Lord be God, follow him: but if Baal, then follow him. And the people answered him not a word" (1 Kings 18:21). Failure to commit *is* a decision.

We live in a world filled with confounding choices and ever-increasing demands on our time and attention. One of life's inevitable frustrations is that we often have more positive options than we can possibly pursue. Sometimes the most difficult decisions are not those that involve right and wrong or good and evil. They may not even be between the "lesser of two evils" or the "greater of two goods." The really tough ones are those that require us to select between two attractive "rights" that may be equally worthy but mutually exclusive alternatives. After all, most people don't have to choose between holding family home evening and robbing the nearest bank! But they often must decide whether to stay home with the family or visit elderly neighbors, whether to go to the temple or work on their family history.

When choosing one activity means abandoning other equally worthwhile ones, we learn the invaluable lesson of committing ourselves to certain goals. We learn to live with the regret we inevitably feel when we can't "do it all." An hour spent pursuing one goal is an hour that can't be used in another, perhaps equally praiseworthy activity. We gain valuable experience as we learn to prioritize our objectives and make commitments.

The Lord's ancient promise, set forth in Deuteronomy, reminds us of our God-given right—and the moral necessity—to choose our own path. We *must* choose; our loving Father in Heaven will not relieve us of that opportunity and responsibility. He has indeed set before us life and good, and death and evil, urging us to "choose life, that both thou and thy seed may live: That thou mayest love the Lord thy God, and . . . obey his voice" (Deuteronomy 30:19–20).

Yogi Berra, the baseball Hall-of-Fame catcher, supposedly said,

"If you come to a fork in the road, take it!" Crossroads and forks in life's pathways are unavoidable. When we choose the beginning of a road, we are also selecting a destination.

Robert Frost's famous poem, "The Road Not Taken," is a nearly universal favorite that addresses the issue of choosing:

> *Two roads diverged in a yellow wood,*
> *And sorry I could not travel both*
> *And be one traveler, long I stood*
> *And looked down one as far as I could*
> *To where it bent in the undergrowth;*
>
> *Then took the other, as just as fair,*
> *And having perhaps the better claim,*
> *Because it was grassy and wanted wear;*
> *Though as for that the passing there*
> *Had worn them really about the same,*
>
> *And both that morning equally lay*
> *In leaves no step had trodden black.*
> *Oh, I kept the first for another day!*
> *Yet knowing how way leads on to way,*
> *I doubted if I should ever come back.*
>
> *I shall be telling this with a sigh*
> *Somewhere ages and ages hence:*
> *Two roads diverged in a wood, and I—*
> *I took the one less traveled by,*
> *And that has made all the difference.*

> —In *Best-Loved Poems of the LDS People*, J. M. Lyon, L. R. Gundry, J. A. Parry, D. Jensen, eds. (Salt Lake City: Deseret Book, 1996), p. 29

Did you ever wonder where the other path, the "more-traveled road," led? Who hasn't looked backwards on his or her life with the always-powerful benefit of hindsight and wondered: What Might Have Been? What If? Or, perhaps sadly, If Only . . .

If we fail to discern the critical decision points, we can— simply by default—drift onto side roads. We may bypass the right path, which is frequently the lonelier, less-traveled road. Yet it is so often the harder, more obscure path that will lead us to happiness and eternal life, even God's life.

Addressing a group of Latter-day Saints during the September 14, 1996, Taylorsville North Stake Conference, President Boyd K. Packer stated, "I don't believe a member of this Church can make a serious mistake that would alter his destiny without having received a warning and overruled that warning." In writing about what he called "the decision of life," President Packer has also said, "If we can be shown where the deciding pivotal choices are, we can succeed."

Amulek did. We can too.

My own experience would suggest that President Packer's statements may apply to nonmembers as well, *if*—and that's of course a big "if"—they will listen for and then heed those inner, spiritual promptings. Although I often didn't recognize it at the time, the guiding influence of the Holy Spirit has been present at most of the critical decision points in my life. Viewing those moments of choice through my own personal "retrospectoscope," I have overwhelming feelings of gratitude and relief. Gratitude that I switched career tracks, finally choosing medicine. Relief that I *didn't* walk away from the LDS Church the first unsettling time I stumbled onto a Sunday School meeting. Gratitude for Ron; relief that I didn't marry someone else.

President Thomas S. Monson often quotes one of his favorite poems:

> *He stood at the crossroads all alone,*
> *The sunlight in his face.*
> *He had no thought for the world unknown—*
> *He was set for a manly race.*
> *But the roads stretched east and the roads stretched west,*
> *And the lad knew not which road was best,*
> *So he chose the road that led him down,*
> *And he lost the race and victor's crown.*
> *He was caught at last in an angry snare*
> *Because no one stood at the crossroads there*
> *To show him the better road.*
>
> *Another day at the self-same place,*
> *A boy with high hopes stood.*
> *He, too, was set for a manly race;*
> *He, too, was seeking the things that were good;*
> *But one was there who the roads did know,*
> *And that one showed him which way to go.*
> *So he turned from the road that would lead him down,*
> *And he won the race and the victor's crown.*
> *He walks today the highway fair*
> *Because one stood at the crossroads there*
> *To show him the better way.*
> > —Author unknown, in *Best-Loved Poems of the LDS People,*
> > p. 313

None of us has the supernatural vision to see around corners and past the twisting bends that often mark less-traveled roads.

We frequently lack both the wisdom and experience even to imagine the full consequences of taking one path versus the other.

If only we could peek! Just catch a quick glance at what lies beyond the bend in the path . . . climb a handy tree or something. Even a map would help. Failing that, what if we could find someone who had either foreseen or actually walked down that road, and ask for directions?

There *is* help. We can receive assistance in recognizing the deciding, pivotal choices in our lives. We can *know* which path to follow.

Most of us realize that our need for divine guidance in our lives is greater today than ever before. President James E. Faust has testified that "by the power and gift of the Holy Ghost, we can know what to do and what not to do to bring happiness and peace to our lives" (*Ensign*, April 1996, p. 2).

Chapter 8

Currents to Disaster

The devastating Utah floods of 1983 were a long-distant memory. They had been followed in quick succession by several unusually dry years that in some scattered regions bordered on severe drought. Faces creased with worry, water masters and other civic authorities throughout the Intermountain West scanned the skies hopefully and anxiously pored over long-term forecasts. Reservoirs sank to dangerously low depths and ground-water levels dropped precipitously. Some areas instituted strict water rationing.

Then the long, wet winter of '95 arrived. Skiers and resort owners rejoiced. Farmers everywhere grinned in relief, then—as farmers often do—found *something* concerning the weather to gripe and grumble about, namely the delay in planting their spring crops. With the plentiful water, golf courses and backyards across the state sported a rare, deep emerald color.

The unusually dense snowpack, combined with heavy, late spring rains and gradually warming temperatures, would soon result in a near-record spring runoff throughout the entire Colorado River system. To kayak buffs and other assorted "river rats," the predicted high stream flows meant one thing: fabulous, world-class whitewater with wondrously giant waves (called "big hydraulics" in river slang).

Ron and I had been eager participants in many river trips. We relished the opportunity to be outdoors with no distractions or interruptions. Fun but relatively safe rapids with scary names like Skull, Upper and Lower Disaster Falls, and the deliciously ominous Room of Doom always provided excitement and adventure.

But in all our years of river running, we had never done the Big One: the mighty Colorado with its legendary Cataract Canyon. Big Drop. One of the largest rapids in North America.

"Maybe this is the year," I said to Ron. "Everyone says it will never get any better than this."

"Let's do it," he agreed.

A phone call to Holiday River Expeditions confirmed the encouraging rumors. The huge, slowly melting snowpack was indeed sending massive amounts of water into the whole Colorado River basin, making this year's runoff one of the biggest ever— perhaps *the* biggest and longest-lasting on record.

We reserved space on one of the earliest available trips.

When we arrived at Green River, the town was full of boaters eagerly awaiting the once-in-a-lifetime whitewater adventure. The patio at Ray's, a local favorite famous for its burgers, was jammed. As we patiently waited for a table, a group of Holiday River guides recognized Ron and me and promptly invited our family to join them.

The guides, mostly in their twenties and thirties, were always full of youthful enthusiasm. This year the promise of record-setting water levels had them especially excited. They were really "stoked," as they put it. Rumor had it that maybe even the Old Man, Dee Holladay himself, would join us midway through the trip in time to run Cataract Canyon and the Big Drops with our group.

70

We all awoke early the next morning, donning caps and T-shirts emblazoned with Holiday River Expedition's motto, "Go with the Flow." With the skill born of long practice, our designated guides—each one an experienced trip leader in his own right—went about their meticulous preparations efficiently. The six huge, silvery, inflated rafts that would be our home away from home for the next five days were loaded onto trailers, piled high with gear and spare oars, and tied securely into place.

The guides explained that the rafts wouldn't float down the Colorado in the customary single-file configuration. Instead, once we reached the river, the rafts would be lashed together side-by-side. There would be two groups of three boats each. This so-called "triple-rigging" greatly increased the rafts' safety and stability in the unusually big whitewater our guides clearly expected we would encounter. *At least that's the theory,* I thought.

They also told us that instead of the usual complement of one guide per raft, there would be a total of two guides for each of the two "triple-rigs." One would man the long oar on the front or downstream tube of the leading raft while the other was stationed in the trailing, upstream boat with the second oar. The linked rafts thus would actually float sideways as they angled down the river, with the downstream side of the first raft serving as the bow or front of the rig.

Explanations over, we at last squeezed into the big vans that would pull the heavy trailers to the embarkation point. Off we went, chattering excitedly about the much-anticipated adventure. Would it *really* be as big, as huge, as we expected?

The first three days, unusually warm and sunny for early spring, were relaxing and comparatively uneventful. The muddy Colorado itself, swollen and silt-laden from the heavy runoff, carried us swiftly through the towering cliffs and eroded red-rock canyons of the river basin. Breathtaking scenery slid by, each view more spectacular than the last.

On the third day, the swift current brought us to our assigned camping spot by early afternoon. We unloaded the rafts and pitched our tents on a solitary plain overlooking the river. After everyone quickly slipped on hiking clothes over bathing suits, some of the guides led the group on a spectacular trail that wound through the grassy plain, up the steep mountainside, and across a high mesa filled with house-sized boulders and naturally sculpted rock columns.

Suddenly, without warning, the blue sky seemed to fill with clouds. In one of those quirky weather changes for which the high desert and western mountains are notorious, a brisk wind swept in from nowhere and the temperature abruptly plummeted. Thunder rumbled menacingly on the horizon. In the far distance we could see lightning bolts crack and arc toward the ground.

"Uh-oh," one of the guides exclaimed worriedly. "Time to get out of here!"

Dangerously exposed on the high plateau, the group raced across the mesa toward the cliff's edge. Far below, a rain squall temporarily obscured our campsite. The gathering storm soon engulfed us, drenching us in cold, stinging water. There was a noticeable increase in the distant river's roar.

Then we heard a muffled whump. The riverbank adjacent to our campsite abruptly gave way, and a huge chunk of land simply disappeared into the raging Colorado, swallowed instantly and completely by its wind-whipped waves. Some of the tents, now occupying prime beachside property, collapsed and teetered precariously over the water. One of the rafts tore free from all but one of its moorings. Swinging and pirouetting madly, it strained furiously against the tautened rope.

The guides ran ahead to secure the rafts, leaving us to pick our way down the trail to camp. Hypothermia, far from our thoughts on a warm June day, was now a real threat. We agreed to alternate walking and running fifty paces, and the group's spirits rose as everyone warmed up with the exertion. A few brave souls even started to sing lustily as we trooped into our makeshift camp. Rummaging around inside their gear bags, everyone changed into wrinkled but blessedly dry clothes.

The efficient guides had already reanchored the rafts securely, repositioned the tents and gear, and brewed up a big pot of hot chocolate. We gratefully wrapped frozen fingers around steaming mugs and sipped the delicious stuff slowly, savoring every swallow.

The rain cleared momentarily, then settled into a persistent, chill drizzle. It didn't bode well for the next day's challenging run through Cataract Canyon. As the afternoon faded into evening, the easygoing, usually lighthearted guides grew progressively more quiet. Their expressions seemed to mirror the weather: gray and somber. They definitely had on their "game faces."

Periodically, when they thought no one was watching, the guides would silently slip away from the cheery campfire to check and recheck the heavy ropes and meticulously tied knots that lashed the big rafts together. Their unusual demeanor reminded us that the monster rapids we would encounter the next morning were no joking matter.

Just before dark, the unmistakable putt-putt sound of an undersized outboard motor broke the evening stillness. The guides let out a whoop of welcome as a small, inflatable dinghy came chugging around the bend.

"Dee's here!" they shouted.

The Old Man of the river had arrived.

Dee unfolded his spare, wiry frame from its cramped position and with a grateful sigh waded onto the beach. He hungrily devoured a plate of warmed-over dinner as he regaled everyone with the latest river gossip.

"She's runnin' right at sixty thousand," Dee grinned as he quoted the latest stream-flow estimates. He meant that each and every second, sixty thousand cubic feet of water were pouring down the Colorado. That, he explained, was about four or five times the normal maximum spring runoff.

"*Yes!*" one of the guides exclaimed, excitedly pumping his clenched fist into the air for emphasis.

"It'll be a great run," Dee agreed. "Not easy, though. The Park Rangers have been sitting in their boats right below the Big Drops to pick up all the stuff when rafts flip in the rapids. Not *if*," he added with a wry smile.

That sobered the group.

Dee continued, "Yesterday all five of the five single rafts that ran Cataract Canyon flipped. Every one of 'em. A whole lot of folks went for a long, cold swim. So it's a good thing you're triple-rigged."

"Can a triple flip?" one of the guests asked worriedly.

"Hasn't yet, although in theory I suppose it could," Dee answered reassuringly. "However, it can 'taco.' That's what we call it when one raft folds back over or under the other. But a triple-rig really shouldn't flip."

I didn't say anything, but I certainly didn't relish the thought of being the "filling" in a taco sandwich.

We slept fitfully that night, the river dancing in our dreams. Its constant murmur, usually a rather comforting sound, seemed vaguely menacing. Fat raindrops splatted on the nylon tents while thunder muttered intermittently in the distance.

The Big Day dawned, still cold and dreary. Dull, gunmetal gray clouds stretched in an unbroken line from one horizon to the other. Breakfast was a miserable affair. The somber group shivered and huddled under rubber ponchos, water dripping from every surface. Our pitifully small campfire, built more for effect than real warmth, hissed and spluttered in the constant rain.

With dishes washed, fire doused, and ashes and unburned wood packed away in the raft's trash bags for removal and later disposal, our trip leader gathered the group together for final instructions.

"Well," he exclaimed with forced cheerfulness, "Today's the Big Day!"

No one cheered.

"I've got some good news," he added enthusiastically as he pulled out some large bags. "We have wet suits for everyone in the group!"

"We coulda used those last night," someone groused, clearly unappeased.

The guides began handing the wet suits out, helping everyone struggle into one that fit, at least approximately. As retained body heat collected under the tight black neoprene suits, surprised looks crossed several faces. For the first time since we had reluctantly crawled out of our sleeping bags and snug tents into the damp morning, we felt warm. A few tentative smiles broke out. Maybe this wouldn't be so bad after all!

The relief was short-lived.

"The wet suits are just in case anyone happens to 'go for a swim' today," the trip leader reminded the group. "These rapids are big, *really* big this year. Even triple-rigged, the rafts are going to buck and rear like a wild bronco. If you get tossed out, it could be a while before you get picked up below, where the rapids end. The water is also unusually cold for this time of year. Without the wet suits, you'd almost certainly suffer from hypothermia.

"The waves are going to be huge, bigger than anything we've seen for years—maybe even decades. A triple-rig shouldn't flip, but remember it can 'taco.' That's when the force of the waves literally folds one of the rafts back over the other," he gestured, illustrating an accordion effect with his large hands.

I wasn't the only one who shuddered involuntarily at the idea.

The guide continued, "If it looks as though the rafts are going to 'taco,' the boatman will yell 'floor!' That means you hit the deck. Immediately. Lie down on the bottom of the raft and just hold on. The water coolers and other gear lashed to the side tubes will keep the rafts apart and protect you. As long as you're lying down flat on the frame in the center depression between the tubes, you should be okay."

Swell.

We positioned ourselves in the rafts as the guides maneuvered the rigs into the current. They drifted downstream for a mile or two, then pulled into the eddy and beached the rafts just above the Big Drop. Everyone hopped out and followed the head guide down the trail to "scout" the rapids.

We could hear their roar long before we could see the rapids themselves. Climbing over boulders, we scrambled up the cliffside to the lookout point.

The first glimpse was daunting. I sucked in my breath sharply at the sight of the roiling, turbulent water. I heard a few gasps of dismay from some of the other guests.

Dee began pointing out the best route through the rapids to the attentive guides. They listened intently, hanging on every word. They all knew Dee had run the Colorado innumerable times, under just about every conceivable condition.

"Precise boat placement *before* you get into the rapids is essential," Dee said. "Setting up a correct entrance is key, as it always is, but especially in Cataract Canyon. Look over there to the right."

All eyes followed Dee's pointing finger.

"That's Little Niagara."

It was aptly named, a sheer waterfall that dropped at least twenty feet into a huge whirlpool of churning water.

"You don't want to end up there," Dee commented unnecessarily. "*But,* it's important to be as far right as you can without actually getting into Little Niagara itself. The big reason lies farther down on the left."

Heads swiveled in unison as we peered downstream.

"A few hundred yards past Little Niagara, way over there on the left, is Satan's Gut. Satan's Gut is even more dangerous than Little Niagara."

We could barely see the top of what appeared to be a huge, spitting hellhole of water.

"You get in there, you might not come out for a while. The backwash is so strong it'd hold you in for a good bit."

One of the guides swallowed hard at the thought.

"The biggest, best waves are smack in the middle, in between Little Niagara up here on the right and Satan's Gut down there on the left." Dee knelt down and drew a diagram in the sand with his finger to illustrate.

"The current will pull you strongly to the left, straight toward Satan's Gut. That's why you *must* set up to run to the right, just skirting Little Niagara as you start angling the rafts downstream. Then you'll be perfectly positioned for the ride of a lifetime.

Remember, the current wants to take you too far left. Resist the current or you'll be in trouble. *Big* trouble," he warned.

With a last look at the thundering Colorado, we hiked back to the rafts, lost in thought. Was this supposed to be *fun?* I zipped up my wet suit and tugged at the straps of my life jacket, tightening it to the maximum. Just as the first triple-rig made ready to push off, the sun broke through the clouds and flooded the landscape in warmth. I fervently hoped it was a good omen.

We watched from the safety of the eddy current, yelling and shouting encouragement as the first group disappeared around the bend.

As our two guides pulled us into the river's main current, we could see the first group shooting through the Big Drops. The enormous waves tossed their rafts around in a gigantic roller-coaster ride. We could hear their whoops of excitement.

Then it was our turn. I could feel my heart thumping and beating rapidly in my chest. For just a moment I wondered what the guides felt like.

Then I almost stopped breathing.

Something was wrong. *Very* wrong.

I saw Dee suddenly stand up in the middle raft, a look of alarm on his weather-beaten face.

"Right! Pull *right!*" he shouted urgently to the guides.

They pulled furiously on the long oars, but it was already too late. The immensely powerful current snatched the rig and sucked it strongly to the left, toward the biggest, most monstrous waves I'd ever seen. Right toward Satan's Gut.

"*Floor!!*" the head guide screamed, his voice nearly lost in the deafening roar of the rapids. I dived instinctively for the bottom of the boat. As I lay spread-eagled on my back, I saw the front two rafts suspended almost directly above me as they were propelled forcefully up a sheer, nearly vertical wall of water. Curving still another eight or ten feet above the front raft was a towering crest of angry brown river.

I closed my eyes as the wave broke and crashed over the rafts. We were buried in tons of churning, foaming water for what seemed like an eternity.

Choking and gagging for breath, I finally opened my eyes and took a quick inventory. I was, miraculously, still alive. All body parts were present and accounted for. Ron was okay. Then, to our horror, we all simultaneously realized that the guide manning the front oar was gone. He had quite literally disappeared. His empty oar hung by its safety strap, clattering uselessly against the metal oarlock. The rafts, now completely out of control, swung wildly back and forth across the raging current. The remaining guide, positioned in the trailing boat, was powerless with his single oar. His desperate, frantic pulling was to no avail.

We were headed straight for Satan's Gut.

"Dee! *Dee!*" six terrified people screamed together. "Front oar! FRONT OAR!"

Dee was already standing up, steadying himself expertly on the bucking, pitching raft as his eyes rapidly scanned back upstream for signs of the ejected guide. As soon as he saw the guide's head break the surface, Dee jumped from the middle into the front raft. In one fluid motion he grabbed the flailing oar, jammed it into the oarlock, and began to pull with all his might.

Every sinew in Dee's neck and back stood out as he strained against the powerful current that was sweeping us inexorably toward Satan's Gut. Water was pouring into its gigantic, thundering hole, carrying the linked rafts closer and closer to disaster.

As the guide on the trailing raft shouted instructions from his better vantage point, at the last possible moment Dee somehow managed to pivot the leading boat away from the roaring hole. The trailing raft, with me and the guide now hanging on for dear life, swung into the edge of the maelstrom, quivered precariously for a heart-stopping moment, and at last popped free.

I exhaled in sweet relief.

Safe but dazed and emotionally spent, we drifted below the rapids as Dee slumped over his oar, exhausted by the monumental effort. One of the other guests took his oar, pulled us into the quiet eddy current, and helped beach the rafts.

Everyone broke into a loud cheer, pounding Dee on the back. He grinned back, eyes sparkling and teeth flashing white in his deeply tanned face. "It just felt good to have an oar in my hands again," he replied modestly to compliments from the admiring guides. They knew that without his quick action and wealth of experience, the outcome might well have been catastrophic.

"That current really wants to pull you to the left. Straight toward Satan's Gut," remarked the guide who had been pitched out of the boat.

"Yeah," Dee concurred. "Sometimes you just gotta know when to go *against* the flow!"

Mortality is much like a river, replete with rapids, currents, shoals, and whirlpools. Mercifully, the rough parts are usually interspersed with occasional flat stretches of water where we can drift for a moment and catch our breath. But we need to stay alert. A wise "rule of the river" is to never take off your life jacket—even in what appears to be "flat water." No matter how benign and inviting the water appears, there are often hazards that lurk just below the deceptively calm surface. And a warm, clear day can cloud up in a hurry, bringing unanticipated chills and challenges.

Going *with* the flow—of a river or life itself—is usually the simplest alternative. We can easily float along and drift wherever the current takes us. Or, as Amulek had done so successfully prior to his life-changing vision, we can even paddle hard to keep ahead of the current while still following its general direction.

But when currents are swift and strong and rushing toward deep holes, there is no time to rest or drift. There are powerful currents that can, if we go with the flow and offer no resistance, sweep us toward disaster. Like the river guides, we must dig in deep and pull on the oars with all our might to propel ourselves away from trouble.

Scouting the rapids ahead of time with someone whose wisdom and experience exceeds our own is a very wise precaution. Knowing and properly setting our course *before* we enter the rapids themselves can prevent downstream disasters.

And when all else fails, yell for help.

Someone is listening.

ON THE ROAD
Accountability and Responsibility

Amulek didn't whine or make excuses. From the moment he abandoned the world's way and chose the Lord's path, he never looked back. The road wasn't easy; the consequences of his decision were often uncomfortable and occasionally even painful. Amulek accepted responsibility for his choices without flinching.

The Lord has made it clear that we too must accept personal responsibility for our actions. Accountability is an essential part of our eternal progression. We make our own choices; we pick our own path.

No excuses.

Chapter 9

The Blame Game

We called it the Never-Ending Winter. It came unseasonably early that year, blanketing Culver, Indiana, with heavy, wet snow in mid-October. Trees still laden with autumn leaves groaned and then snapped under their unaccustomed burdens. Rimed with ice, power lines tumbled down, ensnaring the country roads in their lethal black tangles.

It would get worse. *Much* worse.

That year, winter held the whole Midwest in a tenacious, unyielding grip that went on month after dreary month. Heedless of the cold, at first we children enjoyed the season that the adults always dreaded. We built snow forts and Fox-and-Geese circles, sledded, and made snow "ice cream," a soupy concoction of fresh snow mixed with milk, sugar, and a dash of vanilla.

It was fun. At least for a while. But then the inevitable round of colds and flu robbed us of our boundless energy, leaving us tired and listless. The nearby lake, usually a source of diversion, froze in irregular ruts and wind-scoured ridges that discouraged our makeshift hockey games. Even the local ice fishermen, a hardy bunch who eschewed such newfangled inventions as ice augers, depth gauges, and electronic fish-finders, gave up in frustration.

Christmas passed far too quickly, a mere red-and-green blur

on the calendar. With the daunting combination of short days, long, dark nights, and dangerous cold, we were trapped indoors. The welcome novelty of our new Christmas toys and games soon wore annoyingly thin. Perhaps symbolically, the old calendar was soon discarded in favor of a new one from Easterday's Funeral Parlor.

January was a nowhere month that always seemed suspended forlornly between Christmas and spring. February wouldn't be much better. March was a loss, as usual.

April should have been nice. It wasn't. The trees were still barren. The high, thin sunlight seemed insubstantial, too weak to coax buds from the empty branches. Crocuses and hyacinths remained huddled underground in their bulbs, as if reluctant to brave the punishing cold. Ice still covered the lake. In some spots it remained three feet thick.

Easter Sunday didn't bring the hoped-for spring, either. We shivered in delicate, frilly dresses and beribboned straw hats that seemed ridiculous in the chill winds. The traditional shiny black patent-leather shoes quickly lost their gleam in the slushy, salt-soaked grime that covered the sidewalks.

May came and it was *still* unseasonably cold. I could hardly believe it. School would be out in less than two weeks and we were still stuck inside, restlessly housebound.

Then, in one of those remarkable transitions for which Midwestern weather is infamous, we abruptly went from winter to summer. The ice on the lake softened and rotted. With ear-splitting booms and cracks, huge fissures opened and cleaved it into big floes. In a rare, majestic display, the ice itself began to move. Like miniature tectonic plates, the frozen slabs ground against each other noisily. Then slowly but relentlessly the whole ice pack was pushed shoreward by the warm southern winds that blew strongly across the lake.

The whole town watched the spectacle in wonder. Ice rumbled and pushed onto the beach, bulldozing sand and earth in front of it. Huge chunks piled up in towering, blue-white dams. A few wooden piers and boats, trapped in the ice by the unexpectedly early winter, were crushed like matchsticks and tumbled onto the shore. Fractured boat keels and splintered pilings joined gigantic ice chunks and sand in an untidy, spectacular jumble.

The majestic ice movement lasted several hours. Then, almost as suddenly and dramatically as it had begun, the ice floe stopped its relentless assault on the shore. Open water lay just beyond the jagged piles of ice and flotsam that had accumulated on the beach. The only remaining sound was the sibilant whisper of wind-driven waves washing onto the beach.

Summer had officially arrived.

Several days later, in an expansive and unusually generous mood, I offered to take my younger brother Greg to the town park so we could celebrate our long-awaited release from winter's captivity. He eagerly accepted, scarcely believing his rare good fortune at being included in an older sister's adventure.

We set out, skipping merrily and whistling. I carefully took his hand and led him across the several busy streets that lay between our house and the lake. The warm breeze ruffled our hair and tugged at our clothes as we laughed and ran along the uneven, cracked sidewalks that bordered the park.

Greg found an old can, rusted and smashed flat.

"Annie, can we play 'Kick the Can'?" he entreated.

Still in a happy mood, I assented.

"I'll go first!" he cried, giving the can a vigorous kick.

"Good kick!" I shouted as I took my turn, sending the can spinning and slithering along the sidewalk until it stopped against a piece of broken cement.

"No cheating," I admonished. "You can't use your hands!" Rules for "Kick the Can" were always on a make-it-up-as-you-go basis.

Greg took a mighty kick, but the can, stuck in the crack, didn't budge. He grunted in disappointment.

I took a slower, more deliberate swing, hooking its edge with my toe and flipping it over the obstacle. It scraped and clattered along for a few feet.

"It's all in the technique," I told him with sisterly superiority.

And so it went, each of us kicking and chasing the can as fast as we could go. We laughed and shouted with delight, reveling in the warm day and our newfound freedom.

As we headed down the hill toward the lake, Greg stopped suddenly.

"Annie, look!" he cried. "The pier's been put in!"

Sure enough, the town's public swimming pier stood there in all its rickety glory, arching outward over the sparkling water.

We broke into a run and scampered happily onto the pier, feet drumming an excited tattoo on its gray, weathered planks. At the far end, overlooking the deep water, stood the best part of all: an ancient high-diving tower with an old, thick wooden plank wrapped with burlap feed bags that served as a diving board. It wasn't fancy, but all the kids in town loved it.

Greg suddenly turned to me, grabbing my arm. "Annie," he said mischievously, "I dare you to climb up the tower and dive off with all your clothes on!"

"Are you nuts?" I asked incredulously. "The water's freezing cold!"

"I double dare you."

"Nope."

"*Quadruple* dare you!"

"Don't be silly. I'm not that dumb. You can millionty or billionty dare me, but I won't do it. I'd die before I could swim to the pier. I'd freeze into a solid chunk of ice in a second!" I declared dramatically.

"Aw," he scoffed, "it's not *that* cold. You're just a great big chicken."

I shivered at the thought of the cold water, then put up the final argument, the best of all reasons why I shouldn't do what I knew was both wrong and—perhaps even worse—stupid.

"You know Mom has told us we should absolutely positively never *ever* swim here unless she's with us. She made us promise. Besides," I added with sudden insight, "if I did dive off the tower with all my clothes on and went home dripping wet, she'd for sure give me a really good lickin'. And you'd probably enjoy that, wouldn't you?"

Greg smiled craftily.

I turned and started walking back along the pier toward the shore.

Greg called to my retreating back: "Fifty cents?"

All the money in the world. More than a whole month's allowance. A veritable king's ransom.

I turned. Hesitated.

Decided.

"Done!" I yelled triumphantly. I dashed out to the end of the pier and scrambled up the creaky wooden ladder to the high dive's top platform.

It looked farther down to the water than I remembered from the previous summer. A *lot* farther down.

The crystal clear water was far too cold for the usual bloom of summer algae. The lake was still uncontaminated by the rainbow-hued film of outboard motor oil and exhaust fumes that would slick its surface later in the waterskiing season.

I could see all the way down to the distant bottom and noticed for the first time that it was covered with icky-looking moss and seaweed. A few worn-out tires and lots of broken long-necked beer bottles littered the slimy depths. An old leather workboot had been abandoned in the watery junkyard; its laces waved aimlessly back and forth and its wrinkled tongue hung out in a dark, lopsided grin.

"Shoes and socks too!" Greg shouted up, suddenly concerned that I might actually, inexplicably, really do it.

It was Do or Die. Or maybe Do *and* Die. I wasn't sure.

With a blood-curdling yell to give myself needed courage I ran down the diving board, gave it a mighty bounce, and hurled myself off the end in an awkward swan dive.

I hollered all the way down.

Splash.

The water was colder than I could have possibly imagined. So cold it hurt. So intensely cold it stole my breath. I exhaled sharply in pain at the shock and sank helplessly to the bottom, paralyzed and disoriented. The seaweed, undulating gently with unseen currents, tangled my legs. Time slowed down. Then the excruciating agony seemed to melt away and I felt warm at last. Happy. Peaceful.

Kick! *Kick!* Something deep inside my mind commanded. It was disturbing my peace. *Go away,* I thought drowsily, annoyed at the unwanted intrusion.

Kick! KICK!! It ordered insistently.

Suddenly, I realized I was drowning. I started kicking, frantically struggling to free my legs and push toward life-giving air. The lake's shiny undersurface mirrored the bottom in a crazy, upside-down kaleidescope. I could see it above me, impossibly far away. My shoes and clothes were a dead weight, anchoring me in the frigid depths. I knew I would never make it. Then, with a final last surge of energy, I kicked upwards and broke through the surface, coughing and gasping for air in panicked gulps.

"Help!" I croaked, then managed to will numbed muscles into action. I swam all the way to shore, knowing I was too weak to climb the ladder up to the dock.

I crawled onto the beach, dripping and exhausted. For a few moments I just sat there, panting and shivering uncontrollably.

Greg ran up.

"Annie! Are you all right?" he asked, worry etched on his face.

"Yeah," I answered, wiping water from my eyes. Then I remembered. "Fifty cents?" I laughed weakly.

We walked home, I in my cold, wet clothes and ruined shoes, Greg looking comfortably dry and a bit smug.

Mom's reaction was predictable.

"Anne Gregory Osborn!" She looked at me severely. The more displeased she was, the more formal she became and the more names she used. She was definitely not pleased.

"Anne Gregory Osborn," she repeated. "What in the world happened to you?"

"I dived off the high dive," I confessed. Then, stating the obvious, I added, "With all my clothes on."

"Well, I can see *that*. You know very well you're never supposed to go swimming unless a responsible adult is with you. You disobeyed. You broke the rules."

Vainly hoping to deflect at least a fraction of the blame, I pointed accusingly at Greg, who was grinning behind me. "*He* made me do it!" I protested.

Mother was incredulous. "That's absolutely ridiculous," she said. "How in the world can a four-year-old boy make a nine-year-old girl do anything she doesn't really want to?"

"*Five*-year-old boy," Greg said stoutly.

Mother silenced him with a glare.

"Well, *almost* five," he muttered to no one in particular.

Mother turned to me, waiting expectantly.

"He dared me," I stated part of the truth, hoping she'd let it go and get on with the expected punishment.

"So?" she persisted, undeterred.

"Well," I continued reluctantly, "I first said 'no.' He double- and quadruple-dared me and I still wouldn't do it."

I paused. "Then he bet me fifty cents," I said a bit sheepishly.

"So you did it," Mother concluded, stifling a smile and trying to look stern.

"Yep," I confessed, a faint hope dawning that I might actually escape impending doom.

"*Yes*," she corrected me.

"Yes, *ma'am*," I added, overdoing it a bit.

"Go take a hot bath and get into some dry clothes," she ordered. "Greg," she said, turning to him, "go get Annie her fifty cents."

I smirked.

Mother whirled, catching my look. "Then when you're dressed," she said firmly, "you come right back here for a spanking."

"I'm too old to spank!" I protested vehemently.

That did it. She had me turn around right then and there and gave me two swift swats on the backside. Not too hard, mind you—just enough to sear the indignity into my memory forever.

It was my first—and, fortunately for my eternal progression, unsuccessful—real attempt at playing the Blame Game.

That small, seemingly insignificant episode has become part of Osborn family lore. Greg's children never seem to tire of hearing about it. "Aunt Annie," they plead, "Tell us about the time when Dad bet you fifty cents and you dived off the high dive with all your clothes on!"

"Well," I invariably answer, "of course you've just heard *his* side of the story. Now, if you want, I'll tell you what really happened!"

Then they snuggle up to me in delicious anticipation and I regale them with the infamous episode as well as other much-beloved, oft-told stories about when we were all growing up.

What I never told them—or, for that matter, anyone else—until I wrote this book is what *really* happened. What really happened is that I did an incredibly dumb thing. A small, seemingly insignificant act of childhood disobedience mixed with a bit of greed could so easily have had disastrous consequences.

Small choices. Big consequences.

The fifty cents is, of course, long gone. I spent my newfound riches for some bauble I don't even remember. However, the priceless lesson I learned from that early exercise of agency has remained with me forever. I'm grateful to my mother that she didn't let nine-year-old Annie weasel out of the responsibility for making a poor choice.

Chapter 10

"The Dog Ate the Homework" and Other Not-So-Cool Excuses

Their T-shirts boldly exclaim, "No Fear!"

It would be better—a *lot* better, in my opinion—if their voices instead declared firmly, "No Excuses!"

We are in serious danger of becoming a society of whining, finger-pointing, blame-shifting, excuse-making victims. In the headlong rush to eliminate all politically incorrect terminology from social discourse, some segments of society have adopted the kind of squishy thinking and lax language that disclaims personal responsibility and excuses errant behavior as an acceptable variation within the broad spectrum of normality.

A "Calvin and Hobbes" comic strip that appeared in the 21–22 January 1993 *Deseret News* caricatured the so-called "culture of victimhood." In four brief frames, cartoonist Bill Watterson cleverly managed to incorporate nearly every cliché of the popular victimology movement. The dialogue between Calvin, a precocious young boy, and Hobbes, his imaginary, tigerlike companion, goes like this:

Calvin first complains, "Nothing I do is my fault." Spreading his arms wide, he exclaims to a puzzled-looking Hobbes, "My family is dysfunctional and my parents won't empower me! Consequently, I'm not self-actualized!

"My behavior is addictive functioning in a disease process of toxic codependency!" he continues. "I need holistic healing and wellness before I'll accept any responsibility for my actions!"

Hobbes replies, "One of us needs to stick his head in a bucket of ice water."

The strip ends as Calvin concludes with evident satisfaction, "I love the culture of victimhood."

Many politicians seem to make a habit of displacing responsibility and accountability somewhere into the ether of the passive verb tense. Such comments as "Mistakes were made" and "the System got a little lax" are as close as they come to expressing regret for violations of ethical standards. Commenting on what he calls a "traditional Washington non-apology," columnist John Leo wryly writes, "Abstract villains like 'the system' and 'society' are always available to take the fall" ("Opinions Were Expressed," *U.S. News & World Report,* 17 February 1997, p. 23).

In a continuing legal evolution, increasingly inventive lawyers offer an endless stream of creative exculpations for their clients. *Everything,* even the most heinous deed, can be slickly explained—and thus dismissed—on the basis of one blame-shifting excuse or another. One writer, commenting recently about a particularly vile crime and the defense attorney's strategies, wrote, "Criminal defendants naturally seek to blame someone or something else. They've pointed the finger at everyone from mothers to society, and everything from chromosomes to what they ate for breakfast" (Rick Hampton, *USA Today,* 9 June 1997).

It was no different in Amulek's day. The people in the land of Ammonihah were "a hard-hearted and a stiffnecked people" who "did not believe in the repentance of their sins" (Alma 15:15).

96

They counted on their lawyers, who "were learned in all the arts and cunning of the people," to catch Alma and Amulek in their words (see Alma 10:13, 15).

President James E. Faust wrote:

> When I was a young lawyer . . . I learned that some individuals did not think they were responsible or guilty in any way even though they had violated a law. They felt they were not to be blamed. They had abdicated their consciences. They may have committed the wrongful act, but they felt it was really their parents' fault because they were not properly taught, or it was society's fault because they were never given a chance in life. So often they had some reason or excuse for blaming their actions on someone or something else rather than accepting the responsibility for their own actions. They did not act for themselves but were acted upon.
>
> —*Finding Light in a Dark World* (Salt Lake City: Deseret Book, 1995), p. 61

Commenting on social scientist James Wilson's recent book, *Moral Judgment: Does the Abuse Excuse Threaten Our Legal System,* columnist George Will agreed with the book's central theme, that the proliferation and acceptance of these so-called "abuse excuses" is threatening not only the legal system but society's moral equilibrium and tranquillity. Why, he asks? Because such reasoning both undermines the concept of personal responsibility and diminishes the law's power to strengthen the individual's "often attenuated" self-control.

Mr. Will further notes that in the past, the law assumed that culpability was intensified, not diminished, when an individual committed a crime while intoxicated or caught up in mob hysteria. The law taught a duty to avoid such loss of control. Now, he muses, these circumstances are often thought to mitigate guilt and lessen personal responsibility for crime.

Mr. Will concludes by quoting from Mr. Wilson's book and remarking, "This [abuse excuse] begets a tendency 'to deny guilt, to expect rewards without efforts, to blame society for individual failings, and to exploit legal technicalities to avoid moral culpability.' Thus does doubt about the capacity of individuals to govern themselves erode society's capacity for self-government" (George F. Will, "Abuse excuse threatens society's moral equilibrium," *Deseret News*, 6 April 1997).

Numerous articles on the so-called "culture of victimhood" have appeared recently in the popular press. A sampling of titles includes "Feel Abused? Get in Line"; "Sufferers All"; and "No More Victims, Please." Most of the writers conclude that victimhood has become, at its very least, an excuse for irresponsibility, and, at worst, a rationalization for patently criminal acts.

The transformation of criminal behavior into mere reflex reaction of a victim to some sort of abuse or oppression—real or imagined—makes a mockery of moral agency and personal accountability.

An even more recent blame-shifting tactic derives from scientific advances in genetic research. In an ironic twist on the long-standing "nature versus nurture" debate, a broad spectrum of pundits and politicians are "biologizing" our culture. They have eagerly embraced the concept of genetic programming as yet another way to destigmatize and excuse behaviors ranging from mental illness and alcoholism to violence and sexual orientation.

A recent *U.S. News and World Report* (21 April 1997) cover depicted an infant clothed in prison stripes with the eye-catching question, "Born Bad?" The inside article stated, "Everything from criminality to addictive disorders to sexual orientation is seen today less as a matter of choice than of genetic destiny . . . . A belief in the power of genes necessarily diminishes the potency of such personal qualities as will, capacity to choose, and sense of responsibility for choices . . . . It allows the alcoholic, for example, to treat himself as a helpless victim of his biology rather than as a willful agent with control of his own behavior."

What a terrific tactic! A marvelous new excuse! If it's in my genes, I'm not responsible.

Some authors cite research on twins separated at birth to bolster their strict biological models of behavior. Although some kinds of mental illness may have indeed some roots in heredity, the issue is clearly a lot more complicated than simple genetic programming.

What is becoming increasingly clear from genetic research is that there are many complex, interacting factors that influence whether or not a particular gene gets "expressed." For example, to me the most striking finding on the genetics of schizophrenia is not that half the identical twins of schizophrenics develop the disorder but that half (who have exactly the same genes) don't. It is, to paraphrase Sherlock Holmes, the "dog that *didn't* bark" that is perhaps the most significant clue here.

A person isn't merely the passive result of some pre-programmed genetic code. Genetic instructions can be—and often are—overridden, interrupted, disrupted, and even superceded by a broad spectrum of internal and external factors. Biology clearly affects behavior, but behavior also affects biology. There is substantial evidence that behavior can sometimes actually "rewire" the brain, modifying its chemistry and rerouting its own neural circuitry.

Speaking of accountability and responsibility, Elder J. Richard Clarke once mused: "What about temptation, choice, appetite, habit? *Are* we accountable? As one eminent authority reported, 'Temptation—resisted or indulged—has been supplanted by drives, instincts and impulses—satisfied or frustrated. Virtue and vice have been transformed into health and sickness.' This condition leads us to echo the question of the famous psychiatrist, Karl Menninger: 'Whatever became of sin?'" ("Choice—The Crucible of Character," *BYU 1988–89 Devotional and Fireside Speeches* [Provo, Utah: BYU Press, 1989], p. 99).

The concept that we must submit helplessly to our genetic instructions, somehow surrendering our will to our cells, seems repugnant in the extreme. Come to think of it, such ideas are not just repugnant, I think they are theologically hideous. They are also quite plainly and simply mistaken. If God Himself would not usurp our divine gift of agency, He certainly wouldn't cede it to a bunch of molecules!

Viewing everything as genetic destiny rather than a matter of personal choice represents just one swing of the intellectual pendulum. It too will pass and be superceded by still other temporary fads and fleeting fashions that pass for faith in our secularized society.

Squishy thinking. Evasive language. No-fault terminology. Biological and neurogenetic determinism. These and other popular contemporary equivalents of "the dog ate the homework" displace responsibility for our actions elsewhere and consequently limit our spiritual maturation.

The subtle seduction of the Blame Game can so easily lure us off the straight and narrow pathway to eternal life and exaltation. Moral agency is inextricably linked with personal responsibility and accountability. Our choices often beget consequences that reverberate far beyond the borders of our own lives. Decisions that we think are purely personal almost invariably affect the lives of others as well.

When we disclaim responsibility for what we have done, seeking to excuse ourselves and shift the blame for adverse outcomes elsewhere, we not only fail to learn from our experiences, we may also repeat our mistakes.

The Book of Mormon unequivocally condemns ethical evasion. We are told, "Men are instructed sufficiently that they know good from evil" (2 Nephi 2:5). Jacob severely castigated the Nephites who sought to justify their whoredoms by claiming that scriptural precedents had been set by David and Solomon.

The prophet Alma sorrowed over the immoral behavior of his son Corianton with the harlot Isabel. Corianton had evidently sought to excuse himself with the argument that many others had done precisely the same thing. Alma would have none of this blame-shifting. His plain and direct response: "This was no excuse for thee, my son" (Alma 39:4).

Alma then proceeded to instruct Corianton about the great plan of happiness. He explained temporal and spiritual death, justice and mercy, and the essential role of the Atonement in the restoration of man to God's presence. Alma taught Corianton that mortality is a probationary time, a time for repentance so that the great plan of mercy might have effect. He finally pleaded with his son, "Do not endeavor to excuse yourself in the least point" (Alma 42:30).

Amulek himself also left no ethical wiggle room. The skilled lawyer Zeezrom first attempted to trick him into denying God. When that approach failed, Zeezrom resorted to outright bribery. Amulek rebuked him, saying, "the righteous yieldeth to no such temptations" (Alma 11:23). No ifs, ands, or buts.

In our time, the Lord has again made it abundantly clear that responsibility and accountability are essential to the attainment of our eternal destiny: "That every man may act in doctrine and principle pertaining to futurity, according to the moral agency which I have given unto him, that every man may be accountable for his own sins in the day of judgment" (D&C 101:78).

In mortality, the process of learning responsibility and becoming accountable is mercifully slow. As newborn infants we are neither responsible nor accountable. Loving parents, teachers, and neighbors can teach correct principles and then give young children precious opportunities to develop a sense of accountability through small tasks such as picking up toys and helping with simple household chores.

Permitting children to exercise agency and experience the consequences of their choices is a delicate process. With appropriate and loving discipline, children will gradually learn through practical experience that they are responsible for their actions. They grow and mature as they learn to "do what is right; let the consequence follow!" (*Hymns*, no. 237).

I am eternally grateful to my parents that they taught me—at a very young age—to accept responsibility for my mistakes and poor judgment. To excuse oneself and displace responsibility for misconduct by blaming others is a potentially eternal "fatal flaw."

We may not have chosen our genes or selected our own personal struggles. But agency dictates that how we respond to them *is* our own responsibility. The following poem by Portia Nelson eloquently summarizes the issue:

Autobiography in Five Short Chapters

1. I walk down the street.
There is a deep hole in the sidewalk.
I fall in.

I am lost . . . I am hopeless.

It isn't my fault.

It takes forever to find a way out.

2. I walk down the same street.

There is a deep hole in the sidewalk.

I pretend I don't see it.

I fall in again.

I can't believe I am in the same place.

But . . . it isn't my fault.

3. I walk down the same street.

There is a deep hole in the sidewalk.

I see it is there.

I still fall in . . . it's a habit.

My eyes are open.

I know where I am.

It is my fault.

I get out immediately.

4. I walk down the same street.

There is a deep hole in the sidewalk.

I walk around it.

5. I walk down another street.

—© 1993 Portia Nelson

From *There's a Hole in My Sidewalk*

Beyond Words Publishing, Inc.

1–800–284–9673

Used by permission

Section Five

OFF AND BACK ON THE ROAD
Repentance and Reconciliation

We all occasionally choose wrong roads. Sometimes we start off on the right one and then stray off the path. Sometimes we get impatient and try a foolish shortcut. Sometimes even the right road gets so hard that we feel we lack the strength to go forward. Simply putting one foot in front of the other becomes a monumental effort.

There's no shame in fatigue. Even stalwart Amulek needed to be encouraged by Alma, who "took him to his own house, and did administer unto him . . . and strengthened him in the Lord" (Alma 15:18).

"Give up," one voice whispers.

"Get up, take courage, we can do it together," entreats another, reminding us that the Lord is both the author and the finisher of our faith (see Moroni 6:4).

Chapter 11

Getting Off and Back On the Road

Silly shortcuts and dumb detours are frustrating. What happens if we get sidetracked, if we find ourselves wandering away from the right path? What can we do when we discover we are stuck on a circuitous route or perhaps even a dead end? What if we really are following a Road to Nowhere?

I'm really only half-joking when I tell colleagues I'm quite confident that my husband's only other "Significant Other" is a tall, gangly Appaloosa horse named Chief Joseph. On the high, steep mountain trails above Santa Fe, New Mexico, Ron and "The Chief" have forged a mutual relationship of complete trust and confidence. Relaxed and very much at ease together, horse and rider somehow seem meant for each other.

One year we managed to book an off-season visit to Rancho de los Caballeros, Chief Joseph's winter home in the Sonoran desert of Arizona. After a couple of sessions under the head wrangler's critical eye, we qualified to try out some of the more adventuresome trails that were traditionally reserved for intermediate to advanced horseback riders.

Our last day at the Ranch, we set off with one other couple and a guide for an extended ride into the mountains. Our return flight from Phoenix to Salt Lake City didn't leave until the evening.

We had plenty of time for the ride before we would need to drive to the airport. Or so we thought.

The wrangler who served as our guide talked nonstop about everything and nothing. He seemed in love with the sound of his own voice. Or perhaps he was lonely and was taking advantage of the chance to have a captive audience. Whatever the reason, he talked so much that his monotone and the rhythmic swaying of the horses lulled us into a semihypnotic state.

We completely lost track of time as we rode farther away from the ranch, traveling deeper into the mountains.

I don't wear a watch. I was startled when my stomach suddenly growled, reminding me that it must be lunchtime. A check with the others revealed that it was far past that.

"What time did you folks say you need to be back by?" the guide queried lazily.

"Two, three o'clock at the latest," Ron responded quickly. "The plane leaves about six. We're all packed, but we need a quick shower before we check out."

"Goll-ee," the guide exclaimed, taking his hat off and scratching his head. "The ranch is back that-away. T'other side of those mountains." He pointed straight over some very steep, rocky hills.

"We'll never make it," I said, worried about getting home in time for my duties at the hospital the following day. "I think the evening flight is the last one to Salt Lake City."

"Well, in *that* case, I guess we'll just have to take a shortcut," the guide grinned wickedly. He swung his horse around and dug his boots into the animal's flanks. The big palomino reluctantly turned off the main trail and headed up a little-used, barely discernible path that angled toward the mountainside.

Our own horses obediently followed his lead. *Here we go*

again, I thought, recalling a similar experience in Santa Fe. I just hoped we wouldn't get lost this time.

We didn't.

However, it wasn't long before I would have happily settled for merely being lost. The trail, already strewn with innumerable small stones that formed a loose, unstable scree, became progressively rockier as we climbed higher and higher. The small stones were soon replaced by fist-sized rocks that rattled and clattered down the mountainside as they were dislodged by the passing horses. Then the rocks turned bigger. We were soon winding between large boulders that were higher than The Chief's withers—and The Chief was a tall horse.

Following Ron and his mount along the twisting, steep trail, I simply hoped to stay in the saddle. I prayed silently that our usually surefooted horses could manage the treacherous path.

The horses' hooves clanged as they carefully picked their way through the rocks. Suddenly, The Chief slipped. I saw his eyes dilate with fear as he struggled to keep his footing. Hindquarters scrabbling and straining, he snorted with effort as Ron fought to stay balanced in the saddle. Fortunately, neither horse nor rider panicked, and the horse eventually regained his footing and then simply stopped on the trail for a moment, flanks heaving.

I wondered what he must be thinking. Maybe how dumb these humans can be sometimes . . .

"Maybe we should get off and walk the horses," Ron offered.

"Absolutely not," the wrangler answered promptly. "They're more surefooted than you are. You'd break a leg or an ankle in a moment."

So much for that idea.

A few minutes later, the guide stopped. I heard a muttered expletive. Soon I could see the reason for his concern: The narrow trail headed straight down and then back up a steep ravine. We couldn't turn around, either; there was simply no room to maneuver.

With a shrug and a yell, the guide urged his horse over the edge. They slid and scrambled all the way down, letting their momentum carry them back up the other side. With a final thrust from his powerful haunches, the palomino jumped up and over the top of the ravine.

"Hey," the guide shouted back in encouragement. "Trail's a lot better on this side! C'mon over!"

Ron looked dubious, but our options were limited. Zero, in fact. Looking like *The Man from Snowy River,* he urged The Chief forward and lay back in the saddle as the appaloosa slipped and slid all the way down the steep incline. When they reached the bottom, Ron quickly shifted his weight forward to help the horse scramble up the far side.

One by one, we somehow managed to cross the deep ravine. Horses as well as riders were all sweating and panting by the time we reached the top of the trail. With a gesture of triumph and evident relief, the guide pointed across the valley below.

Nestled in a swath of greenery was the ranch.

Safely back in the corral less than an hour later, I whispered to the guide as he was unsaddling the horses, "Tell me honestly. Have you ever been on that trail before?"

He shot me an incredulous look. "Heck, no!" he exclaimed indignantly. "I ain't stupid!"

Maybe he wasn't. But *we* certainly were!

On that particular occasion we were lucky. *Very* lucky, in fact. Nobody—people or horses—broke anything, but we easily could have. Although we did barely make our flight to Salt Lake City, it wasn't worth the risk, especially in retrospect. Sticking to the main trail, the longer but safer path, would have been—and often is—the wisest choice.

Shortcuts and detours typically don't look silly or dumb at the outset. They often seem quite attractive, appearing as though they would save us time and reduce effort. Sometimes they actually do work out. But they frequently don't. I'd rather not depend on luck.

In mortality we shouldn't allow ourselves to get off the track, lured onto dangerous detours. Elder Joseph B. Wirthlin has likened life to the experience of driving at night on a dangerously narrow, twisting mountain road in a blinding rainstorm:

> I could barely see the road, either in front of us or to the right and the left. I watched the white lines on that road more intently than ever before. Staying within the lines kept us from going onto the shoulder and into the deep canyon on one side and helped us avoid a head-on collision on the other. To wander over either line could have been very dangerous. Then I thought, "Would a right-thinking person deviate to the left or the right of a traffic lane if he knew the result would be fatal? If he valued his mortal life, certainly he would stay between these lines." . . .
>
> If we stay within the lines that God has marked, he will protect us, and we can arrive safely at our destination. . . .
>
> Even though the teachings of the Savior are plain and direct, we are still at risk of getting sidetracked. . . . We get sidetracked by submitting to temptations that divert us past the bounds of safety. Satan knows our weaknesses. He puts attractive snares on our paths at just those moments when we are most vulnerable. His intent is to lead us from the way that returns us to our Heavenly Father. Sin may result from activities that begin innocently or that are perfectly legitimate in moderation, but in

excess they can cause us to veer from the straight and narrow path to our destruction.

—Conference Report, October 1990, pp. 80–81

Most people do the right thing most of the time. But no one, as the Apostle Paul reminds us, does the right thing all the time (see Romans 3:10). Given our moral agency and the precious freedom to choose, we inevitably make mistakes. Some are small and relatively inconsequential, the result of unwise or foolish decisions. Others are larger and potentially much more serious.

So if all of us do the wrong thing at least some of the time, what then? Paul tells us that "by the righteousness of one [that is, the Savior] the free gift came upon all men unto justification of life . . . by the obedience of one shall many be made righteous" (Romans 5:18–19).

To redeem us from death as well as the eternal consequences of our more serious mistakes, God's plan—the "great plan of happiness"—mercifully provided us a Savior who has atoned for all mankind.

Amulek himself explained the essential role of the Atonement: "According to the great plan of the Eternal God there must be an atonement made, or else all mankind must unavoidably perish . . . there should be a great and last sacrifice; . . . but it must be an infinite and eternal sacrifice" (Alma 34:9–10). He then identified that last, great sacrifice as the Son of God. Said Amulek, "Thus he shall bring salvation to all those who shall believe on his name . . . thus mercy can satisfy the demands of justice" (Alma 34:15–16).

Without Jesus Christ's mediating atonement, agency would be—as President Boyd K. Packer has recently put it—a fatal gift:

> I would find no peace, neither happiness nor safety, in a world without repentance. I do not know what I should do if

there were no way for me to erase my mistakes. The agony would be more than I could bear. . . .

An atonement was made. Ever and always it offers amnesty from transgression and from death if we will but repent. Repentance is the escape clause in it all. Repentance is the key with which we can unlock the prison from inside. We hold that key within our hands, and agency is ours to use it.

How supernally precious freedom is; how consummately valuable is the agency of man.

—Conference Report, April 1988, p. 83

It is always difficult to come back, to retrace our steps to a crucial crossroads. But a way back *is* provided. The path is clearly marked and always open. Through our mortal tears we can look to the Son of God and live.

President Gordon B. Hinckley is both frank and gentle when he speaks about forgiveness of sin: "If you've done something grievous, talk to your bishop." Then he adds, "But you can't carry it in your heart all the time. There is forgiveness for you out there. Our Father in Heaven loves you . . . He has great concern for you. Put it behind you. If you do what is right, things will work out for you" (*Church News,* 15 February 1997).

Remorse in right measure is healthy, an essential part of repentance. It motivates us to make restitution and helps us resolve not to repeat our mistakes. But continuing to let regret haunt our lives can paralyze us, crippling our spiritual growth and hindering our eternal progression.

President Hinckley has also said: "When we drop the ball, when we make a mistake, there is held out to us the word of the Lord that he will forgive our sins and remember them no more against us. But somehow we are prone to remember them against ourselves" (Conference Report, October 1994, pp. 64–65).

113

We do need to forgive ourselves. At some point or another we must stop singing the "woulda-coulda-shoulda" blues! A positive substitute is the sixth verse of the much-loved hymn "How Great the Wisdom and the Love":

> *How great, how glorious, how complete,*
> *Redemption's grand design,*
> *Where justice, love, and mercy meet*
> *In harmony divine!*
> —*Hymns,* no. 195

We also need to forgive others. President Spencer W. Kimball wrote, "We must forgive, and we must do so without regard to whether or not our antagonist repents, or how sincere is his transformation, or whether or not he asks our forgiveness" (*The Miracle of Forgiveness,* p. 283).

Forgiving one another is a commandment. "Be ye kind one to another, tenderhearted, forgiving one another, even as God for Christ's sake hath forgiven you" (Ephesians 4:32). And "Ye ought to forgive one another; for he that forgiveth not his brother his trespasses standeth condemned before the Lord; for there remaineth in him the greater sin. I, the Lord, will forgive whom I will forgive, but of you it is required to forgive all men" (D&C 64:9–10).

If we don't forgive others their trespasses against us, we ourselves have the greater sin? *Must* we really forgive one another? On first thought that hardly seems "fair." Requiring the victim to forgive the perpetrator is indeed "hard doctrine." During an intense Sunday School discussion of these same verses, a class member wryly remarked, "I've pondered that one so much it makes my 'ponderer' sore!"

Why is harboring anger and resentment toward those who

have harmed us so soul-crushing that the Savior himself warned, "If ye forgive not men their trespasses, neither will your Father forgive your trespasses" (Matthew 6:15)?

The answer is simple. Those who repent of their mistakes can be made whole again, clean and spotless. The great miracle of forgiveness is that through the atoning sacrifice of the Savior they can be sanctified and justified before the Lord. Of their sins the Lord also promises, "I remember [them] no more" (Hebrews 8:12).

On the other hand, those who refuse to forgive and forget are burdened by bitterness. Bitterness starves our souls and stunts our own spiritual growth as surely as drought withers plants. How others handle their mistakes is their problem; it is between them and the Lord. But how *we* respond to their transgressions is our own responsibility.

Forgiving (ourselves as well as others), forgetting, and then getting on with life is essential for our spiritual health. Along with urging his listeners to get their own lives straightened out, President Hinckley has strongly encouraged us to move forward:

> Now, if there are any of you here who may have stepped over the line and transgressed and think that all is lost, let me say to you that all is not lost. The principle of repentance is the first principle of the gospel after faith in the Lord Jesus Christ. You can repent and you can put the past behind you and, as it were, clean the slate, rub those marks off the chalkboard and go forward with your lives . . . move forward with cleanliness.
> —*Church News*, 6 July 1996

We can't move forward if we're looking backward. Another scriptural name for the great plan of happiness is the plan of redemption.

There is hope. Dead ends don't need to be *the* end.

115

Chapter 12

Happy Endings, Blessed Beginnings

Laurel covered her face in her hands, shaking in silent grief. "My life is in the tank," she sobbed, and I didn't think she was referring to the gas tank.

Ron put his arms around her and just held her while she wept, head buried against his shoulder. "Things seem so hopeless," she despaired. "There's no light at the end of the tunnel. None."

What could we say that could possibly help her? The usual expressions of comfort seemed so trite. Things did indeed look bleak. Her husband's problems had multiplied.

Laurel finally became convinced that both she and the children were potentially at risk, and she decided to file for divorce. That autumn her husband began serving a plea-bargained sentence in the federal penitentiary for what was technically termed "illegal distribution of a controlled substance."

Laurel had three small children to raise alone. The good news was that she did have a college degree. The bad news was that she had no readily marketable skills. Without further schooling, her bachelor's degree in social work would be of little help in a competitive job market.

Other than that, Laurel was okay. I'm not being facetious, either. She had the psychological support and financial help of a

117

loyal, loving family. Her children were bright, beautiful, and talented (in my unbiased opinion). They were doing remarkably well despite the emotional turmoil.

Even in her darkest hours, Laurel retained a firm, unwavering testimony of the gospel. She continued to study the scriptures, pray, and attend church. She never became bitter or disillusioned, shaking her fists at the heavens in anger and complaining "Why me?" She often told us she felt close to the Lord. "I know that Heavenly Father loves me and knows who I am," she would say with conviction.

Her situation wasn't ideal. Far from it. But it wasn't hopeless, either. One of the first lessons medical students learn in dealing with seriously ill patients is the crucial importance of hope. Hope is essential to life. Without it, people can literally shrivel up and die. With hope, they struggle valiantly in the face of long odds.

To have hope *is* to live.

Laurel desperately needed to feel hopeful.

When she finally stopped sobbing, I said, "You know, Laurel, I don't feel sorry for you."

She looked up, startled.

"No, not sorry for *you*," I repeated, emphasizing the "you."

I continued, "Of course I regret the pain and difficulties you're going through. It breaks our hearts to see you and the children suffer. But *you're* going to be okay. The person I really do feel sorry for is your husband. He had so much going for him and he threw it all away. Maybe he'll turn his life around somehow—people can, you know. Maybe he will. Maybe he won't. But you? You're all right."

Laurel looked at me dubiously. "I'm barely hanging on," she replied. "I wonder sometimes if I'm going to make it."

"You will," Ron answered with confidence. "Annie's right. You're going to be okay."

"I remember something my Scottish grandmother once told me," he mused. "She said, in that wonderfully soft brogue of hers, 'Laddie, in this life there's just a little while of everything.' She's right, you know—and that goes for the bad patches as well as the good times. Just now it may seem as though there really isn't light at the end of the tunnel. But there always is. Just keep doing what's right. Things have a way of working out."

Laurel seemed to straighten up a bit. Then her face clouded. "Daddy, did I make a terrible mistake?" she asked pleadingly. We knew she was referring to her troubled marriage.

"Laurel, begin with where you are," he replied. "Don't dwell on the 'if only.' You have three beautiful, intelligent, talented children who wouldn't be here otherwise. I don't know all the answers. But this much I do know: You are a much stronger and better person because of your faith. You've responded to your struggles with courage and determination. Suffering adversity isn't the tragedy. The real tragedy would be to suffer, then fail to learn and become the better for it."

I put in, "Laurel, I'm thinking about your patriarchal blessing. You were probably about eighteen years old when you received it. It contained some wonderful but rather daunting promises. If I remember correctly, you said to your father at the time, 'Daddy, when I read that blessing and think about what I might have to go through to become the kind of person it's talking about, it really scares me.'"

Ron nodded in agreement. "I thought that was a very perceptive insight for someone so young."

Laurel smiled at the compliment, then sighed, "Maybe it's a

good thing I *didn't* know what was ahead of me. I might not have been quite so courageous!"

"Look at the strong, wonderful person you've become. I very much like and admire the Laurel I see now," I added.

"So do I," Ron agreed.

"Even with red eyes and a runny nose?" she asked with a slight smile as she stood to leave.

"Even with red eyes and a runny nose," he reassurred her with a squeeze of affection.

The next few weeks were really rough. When the situation seemed so bad it couldn't possibly get worse, it did. But Laurel doggedly hung in there, trying to endure. She learned to survive one day at a time. At the absolute nadir she said with bleak determination, "You know, if I could somehow magically erase all this pain, trouble, and suffering but it would be at the cost of forgetting what I've learned, I wouldn't do it."

Then one day I sensed something had changed. Laurel had an entirely different demeanor.

"Annie, do you remember when I lived with you for a time before you and Dad got married?" she asked one day as just the two of us were visiting together.

"I'll never forget it!" I laughed. "It was my one brief experience with ersatz motherhood. I loved it. The only hard part was your social life. Three dates in one night! I don't think I ever had three dates in a whole week."

Laurel smiled. "We had such a good time together I was almost sorry when it came time for you and Dad to get married." Then she added, seemingly as an afterthought, "Annie, do you remember one of the guys I dated way back then? A fellow by the name of Lawrence Featherstone?"

"Stocky, blond guy with blue eyes and a really infectious smile?"

"That's the one," Laurel confirmed.

"Nice young man. I liked him." I chuckled, "Then again, I think I liked all the guys you dated. Seems to me you and Lawrence went out a few times but nothing ever came of it."

Laurel nodded. "In all these years I saw him only once, at Kelly Sheffield's wedding. That was several years ago. Then, just a few weeks ago, Lawrence called and left a message on my recorder. Kelly had just told him I was going through some tough times and was getting a divorce. Lawrence wanted me to know he was thinking about me. It came right out of the blue," she replied casually. Perhaps a bit *too* casually?

Laurel continued, "We've talked on the phone a few times since then."

"And?" I queried.

"And nothing. But just talking on the phone together has been a real comfort to me," she finished.

Hmm, I thought.

Ron came home from a stake conference later that evening. After we'd talked about his trip, he asked me how the weekend had gone.

"I had a really interesting conversation with Laurel earlier today. She's going to marry Lawrence Featherstone," I announced.

"*What!*" he exclaimed, startled.

"Oh, not right away, of course," I added hastily.

Ron looked at me. "You mean Vaughn and Merlene Featherstone's son? The one Laurel dated for a while when she was living with you before we got married?"

"The same guy. They hadn't seen each other for years.

Lawrence learned from Kelly that Laurel was getting divorced. He called her and they've been talking on the phone periodically. And she *will* end up marrying him this time," I concluded.

Ron tried not to smile. "And what exactly makes you think they'll get married?"

"I just know these things," I replied a bit smugly.

Call it whatever you wish—personal prophecy, prognostication, or perhaps just wishful thinking on my part. But as the weeks passed, it became apparent that Laurel and Lawrence's friendship was deepening. As friendship grew into interest, they both consulted with their own fathers as well as their bishops. The counsel they received was the same from all sources: Limit the relationship to talking on the phone until the final divorce decree is issued.

They did, and a few months later Elder Jeffrey R. Holland—a longtime friend who had known both Laurel and Lawrence at BYU—sealed them together for time and all eternity in the Salt Lake Temple. It was a happy ending and a blessed beginning to a road that, years earlier, neither Laurel nor Lawrence would have ever imagined.

Things *do* have a way of working out.

It isn't always easy. Although much of the pain we experience in mortality is self-induced, a by-product of our own poor choices, sometimes we suffer adversity as a consequence of someone else's exercise of agency. That which we can't control, we must often endure. However, what we *can* control is our response to that adversity. Will we feel anger and bitterness, or grow in grace, forbearance, and patience? That's the part that is up to us.

When we beseech the Lord for relief from suffering or adversity, He may remove our burdens. Then again, sometimes He doesn't. At times His response to our earnest prayers may be to make our burdens more bearable rather than remove them from our tired shoulders.

The Book of Mormon relates a most instructive, tender example. When Alma and his people were suffering in slavery to the Lamanites, their afflictions were so grievous that they begged God for relief. Forbidden to pray aloud, they poured out their hearts in mighty silent prayer unto the Lord. After He said to them, "lift up your heads and be of good comfort," the Lord reminded them of their covenant and promised that He would deliver them from bondage.

But evidently that promise wasn't to be fulfilled immediately. Instead, the Lord said, "I will also ease the burdens which are put upon your shoulders, that even you cannot feel them upon your backs." The scriptures record that "the burdens which were laid upon Alma and his brethren were made light; yea, *the Lord did strengthen them that they could bear up their burdens with ease, and they did submit cheerfully and with patience to all the will of the Lord*" (Mosiah 24:14–15; italics added).

Succeeding in the face of adversity requires patience, persistence, faith, and a firm commitment to be obedient and trust in the Lord. That includes a willingness to be satisfied with the Lord's timetable instead of stubbornly insisting on our own. The Lord will indeed pour out His blessings upon us, as He has promised. But those blessings will be given in His own way and in His own time.

President Gordon B. Hinckley often quotes from a favorite newspaper article he saved years ago:

> Most putts don't drop. Most beef is tough. Most children grow up to be just people. Most successful marriages require a high degree of mutual toleration. Most jobs are more often dull than otherwise. Life is like an old-time rail journey—delays,

sidetracks, smoke, dust, cinders, and jolts, interspersed only occasionally by beautiful vistas and thrilling bursts of speed. The trick is to thank the Lord for letting you have the ride.

—Jenkins Lloyd Jones, *Deseret News,* 12 June 1973;
as quoted in *Go Forward with Faith, The Biography of Gordon B. Hinckley* (Salt Lake City: Deseret Book, 1996), p. 448

President Hinckley has great empathy for those who have experienced adversity and suffered personal hardship. According to his biographer, his feelings and attitude toward facing adversity have been developed partly in the crucible of his own experience. In his characteristically optimistic way, President Hinckley frequently says, "Things will work out. If you keep trying and praying and working, things will work out. They always do" (*Go Forward with Faith,* pp. 422–23).

I believe him. So does Laurel. Trudging along a correct but long and sometimes dreary path that seems as though it will never end is tough going, for sure. But hang in there! There *is* light at the end. And a happy ending to one road may well become the blessed beginning to another.

Chapter 13

Amulek's Alternative

It was a thought-provoking question our host posed to a gathering of Ron's colleagues and their wives. With a twinkle in his eye, he asked, "If you could have a one-hour, face-to-face interview with anyone in the scriptures—excluding the Savior and the Prophet Joseph Smith—whom would you choose?"

The unexpected question provoked a spectrum of answers, from Moses to John the Beloved to Ruth. I chose Esther, whose courage I had admired since I was a child. Then our host turned to Ron. "Well, Ron, what would be *your* choice?"

"Amulek," Ron answered.

At the time I wondered about his unconventional choice. The prophet Alma was a prominent figure in the Book of Mormon. Amulek, his longtime missionary companion, was mentioned only briefly. Why did Ron choose Amulek? Why not Alma?

"Amulek? Why Amulek?" someone asked, voicing the puzzlement we all felt.

Ron's response was thoughtful. "I can really relate personally to Amulek. All of us are faced with choosing between worldly and spiritual values.

"Think about it for a moment," he mused. "Here's a man who was very successful, at least in temporal terms. In the tenth chapter of Alma, Amulek introduces himself with some justifiable pride as 'a man of no small reputation.' He is influential in the community. He's wealthy. He has many friends and relatives. Then Amulek tells us he knew about spiritual things. But he had hardened his heart against those promptings. As he put it, he 'knew but would not know.'"

Ron continued persuasively, "Yet Amulek eventually chose to follow Alma, forsaking his own riches and comforts to endure persecution and untold hardship. That intrigues me. It's not as though Amulek had been beaten to his knees by life's circumstances. He actually had a pretty good life. And yet he abandoned it, leaving everything behind to follow a prophet."

Nearly fifteen years later, Ron recalled that old dialogue. "Remember that dinner party we attended before we were married? The time when one of the Brethren asked everyone whom they would choose if they could have an hour with anyone in the scriptures?"

"You chose Amulek, as I recall."

"He still intrigues me," Ron replied. "That encounter with the messenger of the Lord was a real crossroads in his life. He could have ignored the Lord's call and continued to pursue the same path he'd been following all along. But he didn't. He turned his life in an entirely different direction. He chose a new path. It was by far the harder, less-traveled road. But it was—at least for him—the *right* road.

"The 'Amulek Alternative.' It'd be an intriguing title for a book, wouldn't it?" he said with a grin.

I smiled, the mental wheels already turning. "Amulek's choice was a really major decision, the 'two roads diverging in a woods' kind," I agreed. "But I also think small choices are important. I just read an article that suggested: 'The choices that make *or unmake* a life are often so small.'"

Ron agreed, "They do add up. President Hinckley often talks about how the little decisions can be so crucial and so everlastingly important in their consequences."

"One of my favorite verses in all of scripture is Alma's plain but profound counsel to his son Helaman," I nodded. "You know the one: 'By small and simple things are great things brought to pass.'"

Ron put on his glasses and reached for his scriptures while I turned my computer on and began to write.

President Thomas S. Monson reminds us that "life's choices remain for each one to make. No choice is insignificant, for we become what we think about. *Our choices determine our destiny"* (*Ensign*, May 1995, p. 97; italics added).

In a world of choice . . . the decisions are ours. So is the responsibility, the accountability for our choices.

An eternity awaits.

Index

"Abuse excuse," 97–98
Accountability: as integral part of agency, x, 83, 100; scriptural statements on, 101–2; developing, 102–3. *See also* Responsibility
Addiction, 37–43; treatment of, 42–43
Adversity, 21–23, 119–20; controlling our own responses to, 30, 122; succeeding in face of, 123–24
Agency: gift of, x; and accountability, x, 83, 100; exercising, in mortality, 17, 23–24; enduring others' misuse of, 25, 122; Satan's attempt to deny, 25–26; crucial importance of, 26–27; requires opposition, 27–28; differentiated from freedom, 28–30; God always respects, 29; cannot be taken away, 29–30; evil as by-product of, 55; would be "fatal gift" without Atonement, 112
Alma, 101, 105
Amulek, x, 125–26; acknowledged "something missing," 1; story of, 6–8; committed himself to eternal values, 16; faced good and evil, 19; accepted responsibility for choices, 83, 101; Alma administered to, 105; Atonement explained by, 112
Anger, harboring, 114–15, 122
Atonement of Christ, 101, 112–13

"Autobiography in Five Short Chapters," 102–3

Baudelaire, 50
Belief, yearning for, 1, 7, 11–12, 14–16
Berra, Yogi, 64–65
Bias, Len, 39–40
Biology and behavior, 98–100
Bitterness, 115, 122
Blame, attempting to shift, 91–93, 95–99
Blessings, Lord offers, in his own way, 123
Burdens, easing, rather than removing, 123

"Calvin and Hobbes," 95–96
Chief Joseph, 107–10
Choices: competing, ix; making, is integral part of mortality, 17, 23–24; consequences of, 24, 92–93, 100–101; small, can be pivotal, 48, 126–27; determining our course by, 56, 127; righteous, may not be comfortable, 57; made by default, 63–64; between equally worthy alternatives, 64; responsibility inherent in, 64–65; imposed by diverging roads, 65–68; divine guidance in, 68; accepting responsibility for, 83, 93

129

"How Great the Wisdom and the Love," 114
Hunter, Howard W., 29

"If only," fruitlessness of, 119
Immortality and eternal life, 25
Inspiration: praying for, 10–11; promised by Heavenly Father, 24

Jacob, 101
Jesus Christ: encounter of, with Satan, 53; atonement of, 101, 112–13; as author and finisher of our faith, 105

Kellerman, Jonathan, 39
Kimball, Spencer W., 52, 114
"Know This, That Every Soul Is Free," 29

Lake patrol officer, story of, 59–63
Lawyers, 96–97
Leo, John, 96
Lewis, C. S., 38, 50

Marriage, troubled, story of, 21–23, 117–20
Materialism, 13
Maxwell, Neal A., 54
Medical conference, colleagues' discussion after, 9–11
Menninger, Karl, 100
Mercy, 112, 114
Mistakes: inevitability of, 105, 112; forgiving ourselves for, 113–14
Monson, Thomas S., 67, 127
Mortality: is about making choices, 17; trials of, 21–23; essential role of, in plan of salvation, 23; likened to river, 80–81; as probationary time, 101

Nelson, Portia, 102
"Never-Ending Winter," story of, 85–87

Oaks, Dallin H., 25–26, 28, 42

Opposition, 24, 27–28
Optimism, 47, 56, 119, 124
Osborn, Greg, 87–93

Packer, Boyd K., 26, 42, 66, 112–13
Packer, Nancy, x
Patriarchal blessing, 119–20
Plan of salvation: role of mortality in, 23; explanation of, 24–25; Lucifer's alternative to, 25–26; is also called plan of redemption, 115
Poelman, Claire, 21
Poelman, Laurel, 21–23, 117–22
Poelman, Ron, 21–23, 107–10, 117–22, 125–27
Politicians, 96
Pornography, 38
Prayers, answers to, 10–11; seeking, 24
Premortal existence, 23, 25–27
Prophets, 47; eternal values pointed out by, 16–17; condemn excuse-making, 101–2

Ramakantan, Ravi, 11
Rapids, scouting, 76–78
Redemption, 115
Religion: as the "R" word, 14; renewed interest in, 14–16
Remorse, 113
Repentance, 112–15
Responsibility: accepting, for our choices, 83, 93; disclaiming, 95–99; scriptural statements on, 101–2; learning, 102–3
Revelation, personal, 24
River: running, story of, 69–80; mortality likened to, 80–81
"Road Not Taken, The," 65
Roads, diverging, 65–68
"Robert," story of, 3–6
Romney, Marion G., 54

Satan: reality of, 17, 19, 52–55; offered alternative to plan of salvation, 25–26; rebellion of, 26;